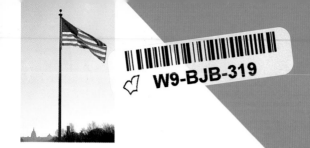

C I T Y P A C K

Washington, D.C.

By Bruce Walker and Mary Case

Fodor's
2ND EDITION

Fodor's Travel Publications, Inc.
New York • Toronto • London • Sydney • Auckland

WWW.FODORS.COM/

Contents

Life 5 - 12

How to organize your time 13 - 22

Top 25 sights 23 - 48

About this book...4

Best 49 – 60

Where to... 61 – 86

Travel facts 87 – 93

About this book

KEY TO SYMBOLS

- map reference on the fold-out map accompanying this book (see below)
- address
- telephone number
- opening times
- restaurant or café on premises or nearby
- nearest metro (underground) train station
- nearest overground train station
- nearest bus route
- nearest riverboat or ferry stop
- facilities for visitors with disabilities
- admission charge
- other nearby places of interest
- tours, lectures, or special events
- ➤ indicates the page where you will find a fuller description
- tourist information

Citypack Washington is divided into six sections to cover the six most important aspects of your visit to Washington. It includes:

- The authors' view of the city and its people
- Itineraries, walks and excursions
- The top 25 sights to visit—as selected by the authors
- Features on what makes the city special
- Detailed listings of restaurants, hotels, shops and nightlife
- Practical information

In addition, easy-to-read side panels provide extra facts and snippets, highlights of places to visit, and invaluable practical advice.

CROSS-REFERENCES

To help you make the most of your visit, cross-references, indicated by ➤, show you where to find additional information about a place or subject.

MAPS

- **The fold-out map** in the wallet at the back of the book is a comprehensive street plan of Washington. All the map references given in the book refer to this map. For example, the White House at 1600 Pennsylvania Avenue has the following information: F4—indicating the grid square of the map in which the White House will be found.
- **The city-center maps** found on the inside front and back covers of the book itself are for quick reference. They show the Top 25 Sights, described on pages 24–48, which are clearly plotted by number (1 – 25, not page number) from west to east across the city.

PRICES

Where appropriate, an indication of the cost of an establishment is given by **$** signs: **$$$** denotes higher prices, **$$** denotes average prices, while **$** denotes lower charges.

WASHINGTON *life*

INTRODUCING WASHINGTON

The Metro

The underground Metro system, opened in 1976 as a sort of bicentennial gift to the nation, is clean, generally safe, and aesthetically pleasing. Washingtonians use the escalators as urban exercise machines, and protocol requires that you stand right, walk left.

Washington is low and wide, with neoclassical federal buildings setting a tone for the memorial core which resonates throughout the city. Architecturally, the most demanding buildings take eclectic *beaux-arts* forms, stimulated by the 1893 Columbian Exposition and the McMillan Plan for Washington of 1901. Earlier buildings tend to be smaller, less showy, and in late Georgian, Federal or Gothic Revival style. Post–World War II buildings incline toward standardized, undistinguished, monotonous presentations marching along the streets and avenues like the bureaucrats in short sleeves visible on any summer day in downtown Washington.

Washington's street grid uses the Capitol as the orienting point: lettered (A–W) streets run east and west, numbered streets run north and south. Wide diagonal avenues, many ennobled and confused by memorial circles and squares, are usually named after states. Two and three-story, brick and stone row houses, 14 to 18 feet wide, line neighborhood streets. Originally single family dwellings, many of these Victorian houses now have an apartment, tucked into a basement or carved from unused space. More people make parking difficult; in Adams-Morgan, Dupont Circle, Georgetown, and near the National Mall, parking is impossible.

The impressive Lincoln Memorial

Spring at the National Arboretum

Washington is peopled by transients who have lived here for decades. They come with the diplomatic corps and stay to see their grandchildren graduate from college. They are swept into the capital city on the coattails of an unexpected political win, and they live out their careers in the shadow of the Capitol dome. They move from New York to undertake political liaison for the banks, or they lobby for the Deep South industries of cotton, tobacco, or sugar or manage associations of lumbermen, airline pilots, toxicologists, women missionaries, and uniformed workers. Since the rest of the country disdains Washington, they are often slightly embarrassed about staying, but they are attracted by the challenge, by the intellectual stimulation, and by the raw power.

Washingtonians take the role of national host with good grace, and they can be counted upon for good directions and leisure-time ideas. This guide skims Washington's attractions, and the reader should plan extra time to explore the sights, stores, and streetscapes alluded to here.

Washington in Figures

GENERAL

- Number of motor vehicles: 224,733
- Number of radio stations: 54
- Number of broadcast television stations: 8
- Number of movie theaters: 58
- Date became capital: June 10, 1800

BUILDINGS

- Maximum height of any building on Pennsylvania Avenue between the White House and the Capitol: 160 feet
- Oldest and largest Jesuit college in the U.S.A.: Georgetown University, founded in 1789
- Largest Catholic church in the U.S.A.: National Shrine of the Immaculate Conception
- Oldest surviving structure: the Old Stone House, 3051 M Street NW, begun 1764
- World's tallest masonry structure: Washington Monument, 555 feet
- World's tallest Corinthian columns: National Building Museum, 75 feet

GEOGRAPHY

- Latitude: 38 degrees, 52 minutes
- Longitude: 77 degrees, 00 minutes
- Elevation: 1 foot (near the Potomac River) to 410 feet (Tenley Town area of Upper Northwest)
- Area: 61 square miles
- Distance by air to
  New York: 205 miles
  Los Angeles: 2,300 miles
  London: 3,674 miles
  Berlin: 4,181 miles
- Driving distance to
  New York: 233 miles
  Los Angeles: 2,631 miles

PEOPLE

- The first year residents were allowed to vote in a presidential election: 1964
- Population (1992): 585,221
- Average per capita annual income: $25,363
- Number of colleges and universities: 6
- Largest employer: the federal government (about 240,000 civilian and military employees)
- Number of federal employees on Capitol Hill: 20,000

Washington People

KATHARINE GRAHAM

Katharine Graham is one of Washington's elite. Currently chairman of the executive committee of The Washington Post Co., she has served at various times as chairman of the board, chief executive officer, president, and publisher of Washington's leading daily newspaper.

Graham was born in New York in 1917. Educated at Vassar and the University of Chicago, she became a reporter for the *San Francisco News*. She later joined the *Washington Post* (a newspaper her father, Eugene Meyer, purchased at a bankruptcy sale in 1933) and worked in the editorial and circulation departments. Her husband, Philip L. Graham, was publisher of the *Post* until his death in 1963. At that time, Mrs Graham suddenly found herself in charge of a major newspaper and unsure of her ability to run it. However, she chose staff wisely, chief among them Benjamin C. Bradlee, whom she hired from *Newsweek* and appointed executive editor. It was Bradlee, with Graham's support, who firmly established the *Post* in the 1970s as one of the country's leading newspapers with its breaking stories on the Watergate scandal and its publishing of the Pentagon Papers.

HAL GORDON

"I was wondering, asking the Lord really, what I was going to do with my time after I had retired when I stumbled over a snow mound and discovered a nearly frozen man. 'Do this,' came the answer." And from that moment, Hal Gordon—retired army officer and bureaucrat, civil rights worker, Christian, husband, business developer, golfer—began learning how to touch the lives of homeless, addicted men and women. Today, the Community Action Group in Washington, with Gordon at its helm, houses, feeds, counsels, employs, encourages and celebrates the recovery and return to citizenship of about 100 people a year.

A Chronology

1790	President George Washington is authorized by Congress to build a Federal City
1791	Washington hires Pierre Charles L'Enfant to design a city on the banks of the Potomac River, siting, according to legend, the U.S. Capitol in the exact center of the 13 original states
1800	President Adams occupies the unfinished White House, and Congress meets in the Capitol, also unfinished. Population now 3,000
1812	United States declares war on Britain
1814	The British sack Washington, burning many public buildings, including the White House and the Capitol. Original Library of Congress burned
1844	Samuel F. B. Morse transmits the first telegraph message from the Capitol to Baltimore, MD
1846	Congress accepts James Smithson's bequest and establishes the Smithsonian Institution
1850	The slave trade abolished in the District
1863	Lincoln issues the Emancipation Proclamation, freeing the nation's slaves. This begins an influx of former slaves to the nation's capital
1867	Howard University is chartered by Congress to teach blacks
1876	The nation's centennial is celebrated with a fair in Philadelphia. Fifty-six train cars are filled with material to be donated to the Smithsonian. The District's population is about 140,000
1901	President McKinley authorizes the McMillan Commission to oversee the city's beautification
1908	Trains are diverted to the new Union Station, which includes a Presidential Waiting Room
1917	The U.S.A. enters World War I; the population reaches 400,000 as the city enjoys a boom

1939	Marian Anderson gives a free concert at the Lincoln Memorial, after being denied the stage at DAR Constitution Hall because of her race
1941	The U.S.A. enters World War II
1958	The East Front extension of the Capitol begins, adding 102 offices
1961	President John F. Kennedy plans the renovation of Pennsylvania Avenue. Residents are given the right to vote in presidential elections
1963	Martin Luther King, Jr., delivers his "I have a dream" speech from the Lincoln Memorial
1968	King delivers his last sermon at Washington National Cathedral. His shooting in Memphis five days later sparks riots; some areas are burned
1968–1973	Antiwar demonstrations on the National Mall
1974	The Watergate Hotel becomes infamous as the site of the bungled Republican robbery attempt on Democratic headquarters. President Richard Nixon resigns as a result of the ensuing cover-up
1976	Many Bicentennial celebrations are focused on Washington. The Metrorail opens
1981	President Ronald Reagan is shot outside his car at the Washington Hilton
1984	The renovated Old Post Office reopens and revives this section of Pennsylvania Avenue
1988	The renovated Union Station reopens
1990	Washington National Cathedral is completed after 73 years. Mayor Sharon Pratt Dixon Kelly is the first black woman to head a major U.S. city
1993	The U.S. Holocaust Memorial Museum opens
1997	Washington National Airport expansion complete; Downtown MCI sports arena opens

PEOPLE & EVENTS FROM HISTORY

"Duke" Ellington

Edward Kennedy Ellington, born in 1899, grew up in Washington (➤ 50). Generally recognized as the most influential American composer, Ellington concerned himself with jazz composition and musical form, as distinct from improvisation, writing, and arranging. He also sustained and supported an orchestra to perform his incomparable music. Upon his death in 1974, the Duke Ellington School for the Arts was established in his honor.

FREDERICK LAW OLMSTED, SR.

Born in 1822, the nation's first and foremost landscape architect began work on the grounds of the U.S. Capitol in 1874. He is credited with creating the vast sweep of lawn and trees of the west front. The Olmsted Walk at the National Zoological Park leads past the animals and gives a good sense of Olmsted's genius for naturalistic environments. In 1866 Olmsted designed the grounds of Gallaudet University, the country's first university for the hearing impaired. At Olmsted's tireless insistence, Congress passed legislation to safeguard Rock Creek as the park that we enjoy today. Olmsted died in 1903.

MARY McLEOD BETHUNE

Daughter of slaves, presidential adviser, energetic teacher, advocate for young people, and champion of human rights, Mary McLeod Bethune (1875–1955) founded the Daytona Normal and Industrial Institute for Negro Girls (now Bethune-Cookman College) and the National Council of Negro Women. Her impact on Washington was commemorated in 1974 with the dedication of the Bethune Memorial in Lincoln Park. As a tribute to Bethune's work for black women and children, Thomas Ball's bronze sculpture, *Emancipation*, in Lincoln Park since 1876, was resited to face Robert Berk's bronze of Ms. Bethune. Her home houses the Bethune Museum and Archives (➤ 54).

A DREAM OF EQUALITY

On August 28 1963 Martin Luther King, Jr delivered his vision of racial harmony and equality from the steps of the Lincoln Memorial to a crowd of 200,000. King, born in 1929, set up the first black ministry in Alabama in 1955 and became the figurehead of a non-violent civil rights movement fighting to end segregation and discrimination. His "I have a dream..." speech was the culmination of a march on Washington D.C. by blacks and whites calling for reform. King won the Nobel Peace Prize in 1964. He was assassinated four years later.

WASHINGTON
how to organize your time

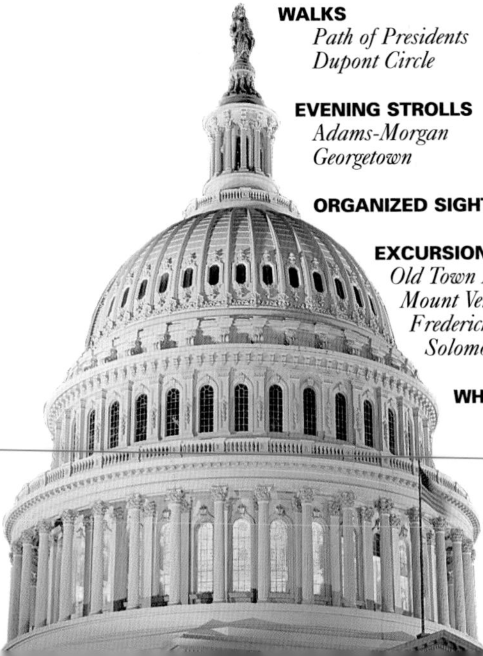

ITINERARIES

Tourist sites and stores do not open much before 10AM. Use the Metro: parking is always difficult and expensive (downtown meters are now 25 cents for 7½ minutes!). The Metro is fast, efficient, generally safe, and inexpensive, but remember that it closes at midnight. Do not be afraid of taxi travel; it, too, is safe and inexpensive. Taxis can be flagged easily in tourist areas.

ITINERARY ONE — CAPITOL HILL & GEORGETOWN

First light Join the crowd of joggers on the sidewalks and paths in the memorial core

Morning Visit the Capitol (➤ 43), Supreme Court (➤ 45), and Library of Congress (➤ 46)

Lunch Enjoy the view and lunch in the Library of Congress's Madison Building cafeteria

Afternoon Walk down the hill to the Botanic Gardens (➤ 42) or the National Air and Space Museum (➤ 41)

Evening Take a cab to Washington Harbor, 3000 K Street NW, Georgetown (➤ 18), the post-modern extravaganza with boardwalk, restaurants, offices, and apartments

ITINERARY TWO — ART, ARCHIVES, AIR & SPACE

Morning Visit the National Archives (➤ 39) and National Gallery of Art (➤ 40)

Lunch National Gallery of Art

Afternoon Visit the National Air and Space Museum (➤ 41) or National Museum of Natural History or, for more art, try the four Smithsonian museums clustered near the Castle, 900 Jefferson Drive (➤ 36): Hirshhorn Museum and Sculpture Garden, National Museum of African Art, Sackler and Freer Galleries

Evening Have a pre-theater dinner and see a show at the Kennedy Center (➤ 25)

ITINERARY THREE — AROUND THE TIDAL BASIN

Morning Visit the U.S. Holocaust Memorial Museum (► 33)

Lunch Kosher Cafeteria at the Holocaust Memorial Museum

Afternoon Visit the Bureau of Engraving and Printing (► 35); stroll around the Tidal Basin and visit the Jefferson Memorial (► 32) and then the Lincoln Memorial (► 26)

Evening Take a cab to Union Station (► 44) for dinner, shopping, or a movie

ITINERARY FOUR — WHITE HOUSE & DUPONT CIRCLE

Morning Start at the White House Information Center (► 30), and after a tour of 1600 Pennsylvania Avenue visit the FBI Building (► 37)

Lunch Take the Metro to Dupont Circle and lunch at one of the many Connecticut Avenue restaurants

Afternoon Explore the small museums, embassies, and stores in and around Dupont Circle (► 17). Dupont Circle seems to have more coffee shops per capita than anywhere else in Washington: people-watch in a sidewalk café then browse in the bookstores—some open all night

Evening Have dinner in Adams-Morgan (► 18) and dance the night away

Dupont Circle café

WALKS

PATH OF PRESIDENTS: A WALK FROM THE CAPITOL TO THE WHITE HOUSE

Immediately following the Inauguration, the president and his entourage descend the west face of the Capitol and proceed in bulletproof cars up Pennsylvania Avenue to the White House. This tour takes the same route.

Begin on the west steps of the Capitol building, overlooking the wide, grassy swath of the National Mall. The view takes in the memorial core of Washington, from the Botanic Gardens and federal office buildings on the left along Maryland Avenue, to the Washington Monument and Lincoln Memorial directly ahead, to the domes of the National Museum of Natural History and National Gallery of Art, and the Federal Triangle complex on the right.

Follow Pennsylvania Avenue, passing or exploring the National Gallery of Art, the Canadian Embassy, the National Archives, and the Navy Memorial. Turn right onto the thriving art corridor of 7th Street, left in front of the National Portrait Gallery and left onto 10th Street past Ford's Theater, where Abraham Lincoln was fatally wounded on April 14 1865. The main building of the FBI is on the left.

Turn right onto Pennsylvania Avenue. The clock tower of the Old Post Office offers an unsurpassed city view. Farther up Pennsylvania is Freedom Plaza, with its incised stone map of L'Enfant's city plan, and Pershing Park, serving as a front yard to the Willard Hotel and to the White House Information Center. Turn right onto 15th Street, past the 1836 Treasury Building, which you will recognize because it appears on the $10 bill, and left onto Pennsylvania Avenue in front of the White House.

THE SIGHTS

- U.S. Capitol (➤ 43)
- National Gallery of Art (➤ 40)
- National Archives (➤ 39)
- Friendship Arch (➤ 56)
- National Museum of American Art (➤ 38)
- National Portrait Gallery (➤ 38)
- Ford's Theater
- FBI Building (➤ 37)
- White House (➤ 30)

INFORMATION

Time 2¾ hours
Distance 1½ miles
Start point U.S. Capitol
J5
Capitol South
End point White House
F4
McPherson Square

Freedom Plaza

DUPONT CIRCLE: DISCOVER COSMOPOLITAN WASHINGTON

Dupont Circle is the heart of single, chic Washington and a focus for gay culture. Clubs, restaurants, bookstores, urbane coffee shops, and boutiques line Connecticut Avenue and P Street on both sides of the Circle, though the Circle itself is home to the homeless. Distinctive small museums and art galleries, embassies, and important architecture are included on this tour.

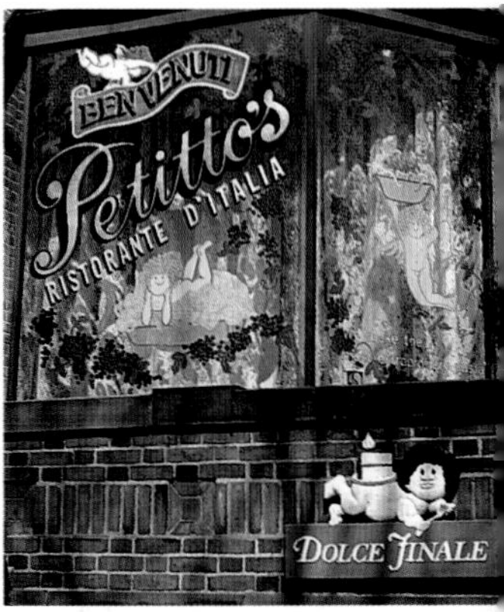

Italian eating, Dupont Circle

Begin at the Q Street exit to the Dupont Circle Metro. Go east on Q to 1700, where Thomas Franklin Schneider's robust terraced houses animate the street. The 1894-built steel-framed Cairo at 1615 Q prompted Congress to introduce height restrictions. Turn south onto 17th Street and right onto the residential Church Street. Turn left onto 18th Street and right onto P to the ornate Patterson House. The architecturally successful Euram Building at 21 Dupont Circle encloses a magnificent courtyard.

Turn left onto New Hampshire Avenue to 1307, the Historical Society of Washington. Take a right onto 20th Street and then turn left onto Massachusetts Avenue. On the left is The Walsh Mansion, purchased by Indonesia in 1951 for one-tenth of its original 1903 cost of $3,000,000. At 1600 21st Street is the Phillips Collection. Continue to 2118 Massachusetts Avenue and pass the walled courtyard of the 1902–1905 Anderson House. In the 2200 block and Sheridan Circle, you will encounter many embassies.

Turn right onto S Street, stopping if time allows at Woodrow Wilson House and the Textile Museum. Walk down the delightful Decatur Terrace Steps. Turn left onto Decatur Place, and left onto Florida Avenue; then continue to Connecticut Avenue and onto Dupont Circle Metro.

THE SIGHTS

- Schneider's terraced houses
- The Cairo Apartment Building
- Patterson House
- Euram Building
- Historical Society of Washington (➤ 54)
- Walsh Mansion
- Indonesian Embassy
- Phillips Collection (➤ 27)
- Anderson House
- Cosmos Club
- Sheridan Circle
- Embassies of Togo, Sudan, Greece, Egypt, Kenya, Philippines
- Woodrow Wilson House
- Textile Museum
- Decatur Terrace Steps

INFORMATION

Time 1½ hours
Distance 2½ miles
Start and end point Dupont Circle
F3
Dupont Circle

Evening Strolls

INFORMATION

Adams-Morgan
Start point 18th Street/Columbia Road
F3
Dupont Circle
Visit in the early evening and enjoy a meal after exploring the area

Georgetown
Start point Washington Harbor, 3000 K Street NW
Best reached by taxi
E4
Visit in late afternoon to enjoy a stroll along the canal before plunging into the shops or exploring Washington Harbor

ADAMS-MORGAN

Adams-Morgan takes its name from the all-white Adams and the all-black Morgan elementary schools. It occupies high ground in Washington and adds each new wave of immigrants to its diverse mix. From the corner of 18th Street NW and Columbia Road, walk two or three blocks in any direction, day or night, to encounter sidewalk cafés, stores, galleries, and clubs. You can eat Mexican, Indian, Salvadoran, Ethiopian, French, Caribbean, and Argentinian. You can dance at the Kilimanjaro (1724 California Street NW) or at one of the several restaurants that turn into lively dance clubs after 11PM.

GEORGETOWN

Take a cab to Washington Harbor, 3000 K Street NW, and explore this exuberant postmodern large-scale complex. You can have a meal here or just enjoy the fountains, outdoor sculpture, and riverfront boardwalk. Walk up 30th Street NW, stopping at the Chesapeake and Ohio Canal. During the day you can walk, jog, or bike for miles along the towpath. Walk a block farther up the hill to M Street, a main commercial axis with small restaurants and boutiques. Go left two blocks to Wisconsin Avenue and the heart of Georgetown. Shopping for all tastes is here.

Georgetown

Organized Sightseeing

GRAY LINE TOURS

Gray Line Tours covers major Washington tourist sites, including Embassy Row. Regular out-of-town excursions include Mount Vernon and Alexandria.
5500 Tuxedo Road, Tuxedo, MD 20781 301/386–8300, 800/353–6114, extension 320 Prices vary with tour

Old Town Trolley Tour

NATIONAL BUILDING MUSEUM

The National Building Museum offers walking and bus tours about Washington architecture and construction.
401 F Street NW 202/272–2448 Judiciary Square Prices vary with tour

NATIONAL PARK SERVICE

The National Park Service produces a brochure that describes the Black History National Recreation Trail.
1100 Ohio Drive SW, Washington, DC 20242 202/619–7222 Free

OLD TOWN TROLLEY TOURS

Old Town Trolley Tours takes in the memorial core and also goes to Georgetown, the National Zoo, and the Washington Cathedral. Abbreviated evening tours available.
301/985–3021, 800/868–7482 Moderate, children under three ride free

SMITHSONIAN ASSOCIATES

The Smithsonian Associates Program offers walking and bus tours through area neighborhoods; often topical subjects—African-American life, *beaux-arts* architecture, public gardens, artists' studios—are addressed.
202/357–3030 Prices vary with tour

TOURMOBILE

Buses stop near most of the sites in this guide, including, seasonally, the Frederick Douglass National Historic Site (Cedar Hill ► 48).
202/554–7950, 202/554–5100 Wheelchair-equipped vans available Moderate, children under three ride free

Personal guides

For personal guides for individuals or groups, in almost any language, contact:

A Tour de Force
Box 2782, Washington, DC 20013
703/525–2948

Guide Service of Washington
733 15th Street Suite 1040, Washington, DC 20005
202/628–2842

Anthony Pitch
Walking tours through historic Georgetown, Victorian Adams-Morgan, Lafayette Square and the White House
9009 Paddock Lane, Potomac, MD 20854
301/251–1765

Photographic guide

If photography is your thing, contact Sunny Odem, who guarantees the best travel photographs you've ever taken:
2530D Walter Reed Drive, Arlington, VA
703/379–1633

Excursions

INFORMATION

Old Town Alexandria

Ramsay House Visitors Center offers extensive information:

- 221 King Street
- 703/838–4200
- Daily 9–5
- King Street Station, then board Dash bus AT2 or AT5 eastbound.

By car 14th Street Bridge (toward National Airport), continue on George Washington Parkway to King Street

By bike Start at the Lincoln Memorial and cross Memorial Bridge heading south 5.6 miles to Alexandria.

Mount Vernon

- 703/780–2000
- Daily 9–5
- Mt. Vernon Inn & Snack Bar
- Tourmobile and Gray Line Tours make daily trips

By car 14th Street Bridge (to National Airport), then south on George Washington Memorial Parkway

By bike Start at the Lincoln Memorial and cross Memorial Bridge heading south 17 miles to Mount Vernon

- *Potomac Spirit* from Pier 4, 6th and Water Streets SW
- 202/554–8000
- Expensive
- Oct–May Tue–Sun 9:30. Jun–Sep Tue–Sun 9:30, 2

OLD TOWN ALEXANDRIA, VA

Six miles south of Washington, Old Town Alexandria provides a good view of sophisticated, small-town America that has retained or restored its colonial seaport architecture and traditions. Start at the Ramsay House Visitors Center, which will provide joint tickets, parking permits, walking guides, and restaurant and shopping recommendations. Old Town, which is easily walked, includes hundreds of colonial buildings, many of them open to the public. The Torpedo Factory Arts Center houses dozens of artisans, often available to discuss their work, and Historic Alexandria, which conducts archaeological research in the area.

MOUNT VERNON, VA

George Washington's ancestral estate, Mount Vernon, 17 miles south of Washington D.C., is the most-visited historic house in the country. The Mount Vernon Ladies Association, formed in 1853 to preserve the estate, can also be credited with starting the historic preservation movement in the United States. The mansion overlooks the Potomac River and is built of yellow pine painted to resemble stone. The ornate interior is furnished with decorative arts and memorabilia authentic to the last years of Washington's life. The outbuildings re-create spaces needed to run an 18th-century self-sufficient farm, such as the smoke and laundry houses, external kitchen, and slave quarters.

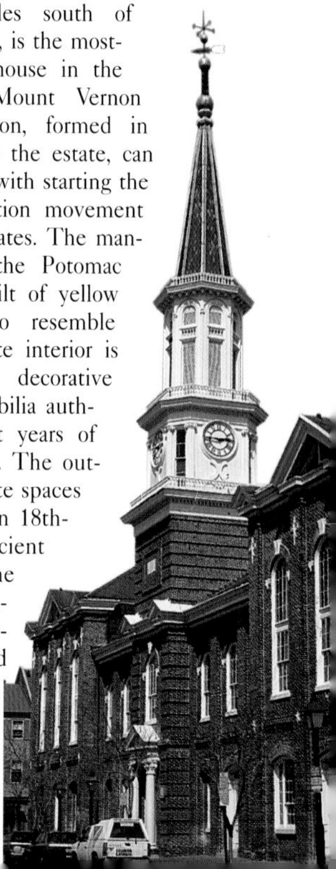

Old Town Alexandria

George Washington's estate, Mount Vernon

FREDERICKSBURG, VA

This historic town, 50 miles south of Washington on I-95, makes every effort to welcome visitors to its 40-block National Historic District containing the house George Washington bought his mother, James Monroe's law offices, a 1752 plantation, an early apothecary shop, and the Georgian architecture of Chatham Manor overlooking the Rappahannock River. Many Civil War battles were waged in and around Fredericksburg, and you can hike the battlefields and nearby wilderness parks. The shopping streets have antiques and rare-book stores and art galleries that support the historic character of this charming town. Start at the well-marked Visitors Center, which will provide maps and expert advice.

SOLOMONS, MD

This area retains much of its rural character and for that reason rewards an excursion, though a car is needed. Aim for the Information Center, 60 miles south of Washington, near the Calvert Marine Museum, which offers high-quality exhibitions about the Chesapeake Bay, commercial fishing, maritime history, and estuarine biology. The town offers a pleasant three-block river walk, where you are likely to encounter several species of duck, historic churches, quaint B & Bs, modern hotels, fishing, seafood restaurants, and a well-maintained wetlands nature park and beach.

INFORMATION

Fredericksburg Visitors Center

706 Caroline Street, Fredericksburg

540/373–1776 or 800/678–4748

Daily 9–5

Amtrak from Union Station. About 1¼ hours' travel time. **By car** south on I-95 to Exit 130A and follow the signs to the Visitors Center

202/484–7540 or 800/872–7245

Solomons Information Center

Route 2, Solomons

410/326-6027

Daily 9–5

By car Pennsylvania Avenue South, which turns into Route 4. Follow the signs for Calvert Marine Museum and Solomons Island

What's On

JANUARY	*Washington Antiques Show* (☎ 202/234–0700)
FEBRUARY	*African-American History Month* (☎ 202/789–2403) *Lincoln's Birthday* (☎ 202/619–7222) *Chinese New Year* (☎ 202/724–4093)
MARCH	*St. Patrick's Day Festival* (☎ 202/347–1450) *Organist's Bach Marathon* (☎ 202/363–2202)
APRIL	*National Cherry Blossom Festival* (☎ 202/728–1137) *White House Spring Garden Tour* (☎ 202/456–7041)
MAY	*Washington National Cathedral Flower Mart* (☎ 202/537–6200) *Georgetown Garden Tour* (☎ 202/333–6896) *Mother's Day: Capitol Hill Restoration Society House Tour* (☎ 202/543–0425)
JUNE	*Shakespeare Free For All* (☎ 202/628–5770) *Big Band Concert Series* (☎ 202/619–7222)
JULY	*Smithsonian Festival of American Folklife* (☎ 202/357–2700) *Independence Day* (July 4) (☎ 202/619–7222)
AUGUST	Everybody's at the beach
SEPTEMBER	*National Symphony Orchestra Labor Day Concert* (☎ 202/467–4600) *Adams-Morgan Day* (☎ 202/332–3292)
OCTOBER	*Washington International Horse Show* (☎ 301/840–0281) *Marine Corps Marathon* (☎ 703/690–3431)
NOVEMBER	*Veterans' Day Activities* (☎ 202/475–0843) *Thanksgiving Day Holiday* (third Thursday)
DECEMBER	*Annual Scottish Christmas Walk* (☎ 703/838–4200) *U.S. Botanic Gardens Poinsettia Show* (☎ 202/225–7099) *People's Christmas Tree Lighting* (☎ 202/224–3069)

WASHINGTON's *top 25 sights*

The sights are shown on the maps on the inside front cover and inside back cover, numbered **1–25** *from west to east across the city*

1

ARLINGTON NATIONAL CEMETERY

HIGHLIGHTS

- Kennedy graves
- Memorial Amphitheater
- Tomb of the Unknowns
- Custis-Lee Mansion
- L'Enfant's grave
- Medgar Evers's grave
- USS Marine Memorial
- Shuttle *Challenger*
- Astronauts Memorial
- Changing of the Guard at the Tomb of the Unknowns
- 49-bell Netherlands Carillon

INFORMATION

- C6/D6/C7/D7
- ANC, Arlington, VA 22211
- 703/607–8052
- Apr–Sep daily 8–7. Oct–Mar daily 8–5
- Arlington Cemetery
- Tourmobile
- Excellent. Visitors with disabilities may board Tourmobile Shuttles or obtain driving permit at the Visitors Center
- Free
- Narrated Tourmobile Shuttle, every 20 mins. Parking ($) available at the cemetery

The most visited gravesite in the country, that of John F. Kennedy, can be found on a hillside overlooking the capital city in the 612 acres of Arlington National Cemetery. President Kennedy's grave makes this a mecca for Americans who came of age in the 1960s, but Arlington shelters veterans from every conflict involving U.S. troops.

History The first burial at the Tomb of the Unknowns occurred on November 11, 1921. This World War I soldier was joined in 1958 by honored dead from World War II and Korea and, in 1984, by a Vietnam veteran.

Under an eternal flame, John F. Kennedy lies next to his wife, Jacqueline Bouvier Kennedy Onassis, and two of his children who died in infancy. Nearby lies his brother Robert Kennedy, slain in a similar act of senseless violence in 1968. Robert Kennedy's grave is marked by a simple white cross and a fountain.

What to see Above the Kennedy graves stands the Greek-Revival Custis-Lee Mansion (also known as Arlington House), built between 1802 and 1817 by George Washington Parke Custis, grandson of Martha and step-grandson of George Washington. Just off the west corner of the house lies the grave of Pierre L'Enfant, now overlooking for eternity the Federal City that he designed with political difficulty and dispute enough to leave him a penniless and embittered man. Throughout the cemetery simple markers march along like the soldiers themselves, many of whom are now joined by their wives. A memorial to women who lost their lives in military service was dedicated in 1997.

2

Kennedy Center

A stroll on the roof terrace of the Kennedy Center provides a magnificent 360-degree view of Washington and the Potomac River, and may turn a potentially boring intermission into a romantic interlude.

History Opened in 1971, Edward Durrell Stone's simple white marble box overlooks the Potomac River and is situated next to the eccentric Watergate complex, infamous as the site of the bungled attempt to bug the Democratic National Committee that eventually led to the resignation of President Richard Nixon.

When the Kennedy Center opened, the space for performance arts in Washington stepped up to world-class quality. The opera house and concert hall, in particular, have splendid acoustics.

What to see The building accommodates an opera house, two stage theaters, a movie theater, a theater lab, a concert hall, and the Performance Art Library of the Library of Congress. Many of these can be seen on a tour of the building or at intermission during a performance.

The building is sheathed in 3,700 tons of white Carrara marble, a gift from Italy. The Grand Foyer, 630 feet long and 60 feet high, blazes from the light of 18 Orrefors crystal chandeliers, donated by Sweden and reflected in 60-foot-high mirrors, a gift from Belgium. Overlooking the theatergoers is a bust of President Kennedy by Robert Berks, artist also for the whimsical Albert Einstein Memorial. The Hall of States displays state flags arranged in the order in which the states were admitted to the Union.

HIGHLIGHTS

- Hall of States
- View from the roof terrace
- Bust of John F. Kennedy
- Painted biblical scenes in the Israeli Lounge
- Henri Matisse tapestries, a gift from France

INFORMATION

- E 4/5
- New Hampshire Avenue at Rock Creek Parkway NW
- 202/467–4600; 800/444–1324
- Daily for tours and performances as scheduled
- Encore Café: 11:30–8. Roof Terrace Restaurant: 5:30–9
- Foggy Bottom
- Excellent
- Free tours; performance ticket prices vary
- Watergate Hotel (➤ 84), Georgetown (➤ 18)
- One-hour tours between 10AM and 1PM

Matisse tapestry

3

LINCOLN MEMORIAL

HIGHLIGHTS

- Daniel Chester French's *Lincoln*
- Inscription of Lincoln's 1863 Gettysburg Address and Second Inaugural speech
- Underground exhibit on First Amendment rights
- Reflecting pool
- View

INFORMATION

- E5
- The Mall at 23rd Street NW
- 202/426–6841
- Open 24 hours, staffed 8AM–midnight
- Foggy Bottom
- Excellent
- Free
- Jefferson Memorial (➤ 32), Vietnam Veterans Memorial (➤ 28)
- Tours available upon request

Fittingly, a century after Lincoln emancipated the slaves, Martin Luther King, Jr., delivered his famous "I have a dream" speech on the steps of the Lincoln Memorial.

History John Wilkes Booth shot Abraham Lincoln in Ford's Theater on April 14, 1865. Lincoln died the next day. Four decades passed before congressional and public support reached a consensus on the design and siting of a monument befitting the nation's most important abolitionist. Work began on the Lincoln Memorial on the eve of World War I and continued until 1922, when Henry Bacon's Greek temple was dedicated.

What to see The 36 columns symbolize the 36 states in the Union when Lincoln died. The names of the 48 states in the Union in 1922, at the time of the monument's dedication, are inscribed above the parapet's crowning frieze. Daniel Chester French's 8-ton, 19-foot marble statue captures a contemplative Lincoln; so powerful and sombre is the statue that one can easily imagine Lincoln rising up and resuming his epic struggles in a Washington still sadly segregated even today. A small museum on the lower level chronicles the monument's construction. The view from the monument steps at sunset is one of the most romantic in the city, as the Washington Monument stands reflected in the rectangular pool created for this purpose.

The colonnaded façade of the Lincoln Memorial

4

Phillips Collection

Washington has distinguished museums beyond the memorial core, including the first permanent modern art museum in the United States, known as the Phillips Collection. Listening to chamber music in these intimate galleries on Sunday evenings provides the perfect end to a get-away weekend.

History In 1921 Duncan Phillips opened two gallery rooms in his Georgian-Revival mansion as a memorial to his father and brother. An enlarged and renovated annex retaining a domestic scale was opened in 1989 and provides additional space for traveling exhibitions and for items from the permanent collection, which change periodically.

Duncan Phillips married a painter, Marjorie Acker, and together they assembled an unparalleled collection of French Impressionists, Post-Impressionists, Cubists, 17th- and 18th-century masters, and American Modernists. They sought out those paintings that glowed with an artist's unique vision; their avoidance of the average lends a special quality to the collection.

What to see The playful Swiss painter Paul Klee is well represented here, as is the master of brilliant domestic images, Pierre Bonnard. Americans Arthur Dove, Georgia O'Keeffe, and Mark Rothko coexist peacefully alongside Picasso, Monet, and Degas. The paintings are hung in simple domestic settings, and throughout the building art students serve as security specialists and are always willing and able to discuss the works of art in detail. From autumn until spring concerts are held in the music room at 5PM on Sundays.

HIGHLIGHTS

- *Luncheon of the Boating Party*, Renoir
- Works by Paul Klee
- *Repentant Peter*, El Greco
- *Entrance to the Public Garden at Arles*, Van Gogh
- *Dancers at the Bar*, Degas
- American Modernists
- Pierre Bonnard collection

INFORMATION

- E3
- 1600–1612 21st Street NW
- 202/387–2151
- Tue–Sat 10–5; Sun 12–7; also Thu 5–8
- Café
- Dupont Circle
- Excellent
- Moderate Sat, Sun; contributions Mon–Fri
- Tours Wed and Sat 2PM

Top: Luncheon of the Boating Party *by Pierre Auguste Renoir (1881)*

5

Vietnam Veterans Memorial

HIGHLIGHTS

- Inscribed names
- Frederick Hart's sculptural group
- Glenna Goodacre's sculptural group
- The city reflected in the polished stone

INFORMATION

- E5
- Near Constitution Avenue between 21st and 22nd Streets, NW
- 202/634–1568
- Open 24 hours, staffed 8AM–midnight
- Foggy Bottom
- Excellent
- Free
- Presidents' Monuments (➤ 26, 31, 32); Albert Einstein Memorial (➤ 57)
- Rangers available to assist in locating names and to provide paper and graphite suitable for taking an imprint of the names

Names on the Wall

The Vietnam Veterans Memorial has been called the most moving memorial in Washington, and on most days there is an almost constant procession of quiet visitors moving down into the "black gash of shame," as one veteran characterized it.

History Maya Ying Lin's design is simplicity itself: two triangular stone walls set at a 125-degree angle and sited between the Washington Monument and Lincoln Memorial. At its apex the walls taper to 10 feet in height and seem to overpower the visitors standing beneath them. The names of heroes who made the ultimate sacrifice for their country are placed chronologically: more than 58,000 killed or missing in action from 1956 to 1975, the longest war in American history.

What to see The polished black granite reflects sky, trees, nearby monuments, and the faces of visitors as they search for the names of fathers, sons, and loved ones. Each day National Park Service Rangers collect the mementoes left near a soldier's name: letters, uniforms, military emblems, and photographs. These tokens receive the care of museum acquisitions and are held by the National Park Service in perpetuity as part of the history of the nation.

The Wall, as it is commonly called, was thought by some veterans insufficient to represent them. In 1984 Frederick Hart's slightly larger-than-life sculpture of three soldiers was dedicated, sited at one of the entrances to the Wall. The Vietnam Veterans Women's Memorial—a figural sculpture by Glenna Goodacre—was dedicated nearby on Veterans' Day, 1993.

6

NATIONAL GEOGRAPHIC SOCIETY

Walk into any international company's Washington office and you are likely to see a 6-foot-high map of the world pinned with the locations of the missions, projects, and plants of the enterprise. These maps, an affectation of the frequent-flyer set, invariably come from the National Geographic Society.

History Since 1888 the Society has increased and diffused geographic knowledge as directed by its charter. Even today, the familiar yellow monthly *National Geographic* magazine may be the first current information about life around the world that many American schoolchildren receive.

What to see Explorers Hall is located on the first floor of Edward Durrell's glass-and-marble 10-story building. Architectural buffs notice the similarities to the Kennedy Center, also designed by Durrell. *Geographica*, a high-tech, celebratory exhibit installed for National Geo's centennial in 1988, allows you to touch a tornado, explore a Martian landscape, test your knowledge of early human development, investigate undersea archaeology, and gawk at space trivia. The world's largest freestanding globe, 11 feet tall and 34 feet in circumference, shows Earth at a scale of 1 inch to 60 miles. There are short films, one narrated by Leonard Nimoy of *Star Trek* fame, and an interactive amphitheater that simulates orbital flight and looks at Earth from space. Exhibits are enhanced by exquisite, large-format images taken by the Society's award-winning photographers. In the gift shop, you can buy the Society's many publications: maps, books, videos, and CD-ROMs.

HIGHLIGHTS

- World's largest freestanding globe
- Touch a tornado
- Earth Station One
- Holographic images
- Rock and water courtyard
- Model of Jacques Cousteau's diving saucer
- Admiral Robert E. Perry's dogsled
- Moon rock
- National Geo T.V. Room

INFORMATION

- F3
- 17th and M Streets NW
- 202/857–7588
- Mon–Sat 9–5; Sun 10–5
- Dupont Circle, Farragut North
- Excellent
- Free

7

THE WHITE HOUSE

HIGHLIGHTS

- *Abraham Lincoln,* G. P. A. Healy
- Jacqueline Kennedy Rose Garden
- French and English gilded silver
- East Room
- *George Washington,* Gilbert Stuart

INFORMATION

- F4
- 1600 Pennsylvania Avenue
- 202/456–7041
- Tue–Sat 10AM–noon
- McPherson Square, Metro Center
- Excellent
- Free
- For free timed tickets and historical exhibitions, go to the White House Information Center in the Department of Commerce Building, 15th and H Streets NW. Arrive at the White House Information Center by 8AM for a chance of tickets that day

Virtually every desk, tea service, silver platter, decanter, painting, and floor covering in the house intertwines with the historic events, writ large and small, of the American democracy.

History Despite the fact that Thomas Jefferson called James Hogan's original design "big enough for two emperors, one Pope, and the grand Lama," when he became the second occupant of 1600 Pennsylvania Avenue in 1801, Jefferson designed and added colonnaded wings to house domestic and office functions. Today the White House looks modest, flanked as it is by the U.S. Treasury, the largest Greek-Revival building anywhere in the world, and the 10-acre Old Executive Office Building, memorably described by President Harry Truman as "the greatest monstrosity in America." The British burned the White House in 1814, and the rebuilding that followed was only one of several renovations conducted over the years by First Families.

What to see Each occupant has left his mark so that, today the president's house holds an impressive display of decorative arts from the Sheraton, French and American Empire, Queen Anne, and Federal periods. There are carved Carrara marble mantels, Bohemian cut-glass chandeliers, Turkish Hereke carpets, and elaborate plasterwork throughout, as well as 18 acres of gardens. The exact program of a White House tour may vary because of the conduct of official business. Usually open to visitors are the ceremonial East Room, a small drawing-room known as the Green Room, the Blue and Red Rooms (known for their superb French Empire furnishings), and the neoclassical State Dining Room.

8

WASHINGTON MONUMENT

Children, in particular, enjoy the 70-second ride to the pinnacle of this, the highest structure in Washington, where a wide perspective on the District, Maryland, and Virginia can be gained.

History The Washington Monument punctuates the axis of the White House and Jefferson Memorial and the U.S. Congress and Lincoln Memorial, a perfect example of how government projects can go awry. A 1783 Congressional resolution called for an equestrian statue to honor George Washington for his heroic leadership during the American Revolution. Nothing happened until 1836, when private citizens formed the Washington National Monument Society and solicited one dollar from every living American. Having raised $28,000, the group laid the cornerstone to Robert Mills's design in 1848. The Civil War interrupted work on the obelisk; construction did not resume until the national fervor surrounding the Centennial of the American Revolution in 1876. The interruption is evident in the change in the marble's color 150 feet from the ground.

What to see Five hundred and fifty-five feet, five-and-a-half inches, of marble obelisk comprise the monument. The view from the top encompasses most of the District and parts of Maryland and Virginia: spy out the Tidal Basin, the Jefferson and Lincoln memorials, the White House, the U.S. Capitol, the Library of Congress, and the Smithsonian Institution. Visitors who take the guided walk down the monument's 898 steps, instead of going down in the elevator, can see the commemorative plaques donated during construction by states, masonic lodges, church groups, and foreign countries. Lines tend to be shorter at night.

HIGHLIGHTS

- Views from the top
- Plaques

INFORMATION

- F5/G5
- The Mall at 15th Street NW
- 202/426–6840
- Apr–Labor Day daily 8AM–midnight. Labor Day–Mar daily 9–5. Last elevators 11:45.M, 4:45PM
- Smithsonian
- Excellent
- Free
- Smithsonian Institution (➤ 36), Memorials (➤ 26, 28, 32)
- Timed tickets distributed daily at 8:30AM and through Ticketmaster ☎ 202/432–7328 Guided tours Sat, Sun 10, 2

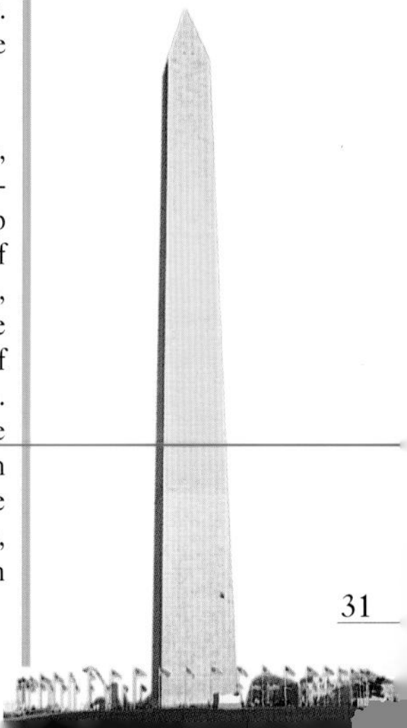

JEFFERSON MEMORIAL

HIGHLIGHTS

- Jefferson bronze
- Inscribed Declaration of Independence
- Jefferson's statement on the separation of church and state
- Japanese lantern on Kurtz Bridge
- Exhibit on Jefferson's inventions
- Cherry blossoms in April

INFORMATION

- F6
- South bank of the Tidal Basin
- 202/426–6821
- Daily 8AM–midnight
- Smithsonian Metro (20-minute walk)
- Excellent
- Free

The Tidal Basin

MNMT VW. Freshmen members of Congress decipher these letters in the classified section of **The Washington Post** *when choosing a place to live: Monument View. Washington orients by the memorials.*

History The Jefferson Memorial forms a north–south axis with the White House and, like virtually all building projects in Washington, it caused controversy in the capital city. John Russell Pope's design adapted Rome's Pantheon in deference to Jefferson's love of classical architecture. Jefferson, an amateur architect himself, had used similar circular domed structures at his home, Monticello, and at the University of Virginia. But Pope's design was derided as antique by important Washingtonians. Others argued that Jefferson's philosophy dictated a more utilitarian structure, perhaps an amphitheater. Eventually, Pope's design was dedicated in 1943 on Jefferson's 200th birthday.

What to see A wide plaza overlooks the Tidal Basin, and formal stairs lead up through a pedimented portico, surrounded by an Ionic colonnade encircling the open center. The pediment supports sculpted marble figures of Jefferson, Benjamin Franklin, John Adams, Roger Sherman, and Robert Livingston, members of the Constitution-drafting committee. Rudolph Evans produced the 19-foot bronze sculpture of Jefferson standing in the center, which is surrounded by excerpts of his speeches and writings carved into the walls. In April, blossoming cherry trees frame the memorial.

10

U.S. Holocaust Memorial Museum

This museum sets new standards for museum design, historical interpretation, functional architecture, and visitor services. To almost everyone's surprise, however, the museum continues to be oversubscribed, and visitors require timed tickets.

History "You cannot deal with the Holocaust as a reasonable thing," explained architect James Ingo Freed. To that end, he created a discordant building, dedicated in 1993, intended to disturb the classical façades and placid faces seen everywhere in Washington.

What to see Watchtowers line the north and south walls and contribute to the prisonlike atmosphere of the building. This prevails throughout, in the exposed beams, metal railings, and malevolent elevators. Everywhere one looks or stands there is a memory or a nightmare that has never before surfaced in a public place. The museum tells the story of 11 million of the world's citizens killed by the Nazis between 1933 and 1945. This is a story not of war, but of human nature itself gone berserk. In so far as possible, the victims and the survivors relate their experiences directly. You will find yourself horrified and shocked but compelled to continue, and grateful when provided with a place to rest and reflect. The Hall of Remembrance on the ground floor provides just such a space, with filtered light and soaring stonework transforming the museum from historic monument to place of spiritual solace. The implicit question posed by the museum is not, Why did it happen? but, How do we prevent similar occurrences? Thinking deeply about this question is perhaps the challenge of the visit.

HIGHLIGHTS

- Main exhibition
- Hall of Remembrance
- Hall of Witness
- Works of art
- For children over 12: *Daniel's Story*

INFORMATION

- G5
- 14th Street and Wallenberg Place SW. South of Independence
- 202/488–0400, Ticketmaster 202/432–SEAT, 800/551–SEAT
- Daily 10–5:30
- Kosher restaurant
- Smithsonian
- Excellent
- Free
- Presidents' Memorials (➤ 26, 31, 32), Smithsonian Institution (➤ 36), Bureau of Engraving and Printing (➤ 35)
- Timed tickets distributed at 10AM daily; advance tickets through Ticketmaster 202/432–7328, 800/551–7328; line up early (before 9AM) or book two weeks in advance.

National Museum of American History

HIGHLIGHTS

- The Star Spangled Banner
- Statue of George Washington by Horatio Greenough
- Hands-on-History Room
- Hands-on-Science Room
- *John Bull*
- Muhammed Ali's boxing gloves
- Ruby slippers from the *Wizard of Oz*

INFORMATION

- G5
- Constitution Avenue and 14th Street NW
- 202/357–2700
- Daily 10–5:30
- Cafeteria
- Smithsonian, Federal Triangle
- Excellent
- Free
- Smithsonian Institution (➤ 36), U.S. Holocaust Memorial Museum (➤ 33), Bureau of Engraving and Printing (➤ 35)
- Tours available

Here is told the story of all the American people. From the Star Spangled Banner to Judy Garland's ruby slippers to Duke Ellington's papers to the gowns worn by First Ladies at inaugural balls, here are the objects that tell of life in America.

What to see The museum mounts exhibits depicting events and themes that define American life. Among these, "Field to Factory" tells the story of African-Americans migrating from the rural, agricultural South to northern industrial cities. "A More Perfect Union" contributes to the ongoing dialogue about the American Constitution by depicting the withdrawing of civil liberties from Japanese Americans during World War II. The largest exhibition ever mounted is "The Information Age," rich in automated gear ranging from early telephones to robotics to high-definition television. "From Parlor to Politics" and "First Ladies: Political Role and Public Image" depict women's political impact. Big exhibits on the Industrial Revolution and "Science in American Life" round out the offerings. Post your cards in the original West Virginia general store; get your picture taken in front of the 280-ton steam engine *John Bull*, the oldest working locomotive in the country; and have an old-fashioned float in the ice cream parlor.

George Washington as a Greek god

12

BUREAU OF ENGRAVING & PRINTING

Nondescript government buildings rarely attract the attention of visitors. Here at the Bureau of Engraving and Printing, however, children and adults alike take pleasure in watching the powerful printing presses turn out over $20 million every day.

History The Bureau moved to this site back in 1930 from the redbrick Auditor's Building still standing on the corner, and prints all U.S. currency, stamps, presidential invitations, and military certificates. Federal presses produce a staggering $100 billion annually, in addition to 30 billion postage stamps. If the printing process goes even slightly awry and produces imperfect bills, the coveted greenbacks are summarily shredded. Also here is the grandly titled Office of Mutilated Currency, where citizens go to redeem bills partially destroyed by fire, flood or laundry mishaps.

What to see Visitors see a film on the history of currency and file past processing rooms where over $20 million a day are produced. The printing room produces giant currency sheets, each holding 32 bills. The sheets are then trimmed, stacked, and bundled for distribution to the Federal Reserve Banks across the nation. The self-guided, 20-minute tour ends at an exhibition hall that contains informative displays on the history of currency, counterfeiting, and stamps.

Do not be daunted by the lines: they move rapidly. Outside, you'll find yourself near the Tidal Basin, with its paddle boats and tree-lined pathways strewn with petals from the cherry trees in early spring. This is one of the most beautiful sights the city has to offer.

HIGHLIGHTS

- View of the Tidal Basin
- Presses printing dollars
- Film on the history of currency
- Exhibition on stamps
- Stacks of money, bundled for shipping

INFORMATION

- G6
- 14 and C Streets SW
- 202/874–3019
- All year Mon–Fri 9–2. Closed Dec 25
- Smithsonian
- Excellent
- Free
- U.S. Holocaust Memorial Museum (➤ 33)
- Guided tours. Tickets required Apr–Sep. Available at Wallenberg Place

13

SMITHSONIAN INSTITUTION

HIGHLIGHTS

Mall museums

- Arts and Industries Building
- Arthur M. Sackler Gallery
- Freer Gallery of Art
- Hirshhorn Museum and Sculpture Garden
- National Air and Space Museum (➤ 41)
- National Gallery of Art (East and West Wings) (➤ 40)
- National Museum of African Art
- National Museum of American History (➤ 34)
- National Museum of Natural History

Museums off the Mall

- Anacostia Museum
- National Museum of American Art (➤ 38)
- National Portrait Gallery (➤ 38)
- National Postal Museum
- National Zoological Park (➤ 53)
- Renwick Gallery

INFORMATION

- G5/H5
- Jefferson Drive at 10th Street SW
- 202/357–2700
- Daily 10:00–5:30
- The Commons for Smithsonian Members
- Smithsonian
- Excellent
- Free
- Film every 20 mins

Tourists streaming off Metro escalators on a summer morning frequently ask briefcase-toting commuters, "Where is the Smithsonian?" There is usually a suspicious silence when the local answers: "Everything you see is the Smithsonian."

History An Englishman, James Smithson, stipulated that his estate should go "to the United States of America, to found at Washington, under the name of the Smithsonian Institution an Establishment for the increase and diffusion of knowledge." After typical political wrangling, John Quincy Adams convinced Congress to take the gift, which was worth about $515,000 when it was accepted in 1846. Today there are 15 museums and the national zoo, 140 million objects and specimens, countless research projects in almost every country on earth, 6,000 employees, and an annual budget of nearly $400 million.

What to see Start your visit at James Renwick's 1855 turreted, asymmetrical, red-sandstone "Castle," recently renovated into a visitor information center. The Castle staff, mostly volunteers, are multilingual, as are many brochures, interactive maps, and touch-screen programs, all designed to assist visitors to the Smithsonian and to other Washington sights.

The different museums of the Institute are mainly on both sides of the Mall, between 3rd and 14th Streets. Research is conducted on Russian voles, Native American baskets, endangered insects of the rain forests, aerodynamics, molecular biology, metallurgy, linguistics, political science, ancient foodways, textile manufacture—and these topics are only the ones that come immediately to mind.

14

FBI BUILDING

Most Americans are law-abiding citizens, but nothing fascinates them more than crime and crime prevention. The FBI Building is on most children's lists of "ten most wanted" things to do in the District.

History Stanley Gladych's modern, poured-concrete building in the New Brutalism school of architecture conjures Big Brother looming half-way between the Capitol and the White House on Pennsylvania Avenue. Eight thousand federal employees operate out of the city-block square, which embodies the "idea of a central core of files." The FBI is the supreme federal authority on domestic crime, having grown from an investigative force chartered in 1908, and it deals with terrorism, organized crime, and industrial espionage, among much else. Even today, the FBI is instilled with the values of its most famous director, J. Edgar Hoover, who ran the agency from 1928 to 1972, an astounding 44 years. FBI agents remain the most respected investigative force in America, and their headquarters is one of the most popular tourist attractions in Washington: be prepared for lines.

What to see The tour takes in historical exhibits about famous cases the FBI has solved, an introduction to laboratory work including DNA analysis of hair fibers and blood samples, fingerprint matching, and a live-ammunition firearms demonstration followed by a question and answer session. Be alert when you visit: two of the FBI's most-wanted characters were fingered by tourists who saw the "Wanted" posters while on the tour.

HIGHLIGHTS

- Live-ammo demonstration
- FBI Most Wanted files
- FBI Most Famous Cases
- Exhibition of FBI history
- Insight into the lives and training of FBI agents

INFORMATION

- G5
- E and 9th Streets NW
- 202/324–3447
- Mon–Fri 8:45–4:15
- Federal Triangle
- Excellent
- Free
- Smithsonian Institution (➤ 36), Ford's Theater (➤ 78)
- Tours every 20 mins

FBI crest

15

AMERICAN ART & PORTRAIT GALLERIES

HIGHLIGHTS

The National Portrait Gallery

- *Thomas Jefferson* and *George and Martha Washington* by Gilbert Stuart
- Works by Mary Cassatt and John Singleton Copley
- Paintings of Native Americans by George Catlin
- Photographs of sports figures

The National Museum of American Art

- *The Spiral,* Alexander Calder
- *Throne of the Third Heaven of the Nations' Millennium General Assembly,* James Hampton
- Ash Can School paintings
- *The Chasm of the Colorado* and *The Grand Canyon of the Yellowstone,* Thomas Moran

INFORMATION

- H4
- Old Patent Office Building, 8th and F Streets NW
- 202/357–2700
- Daily 10–5:30
- Patent Pending
- Gallery Place
- Excellent
- Free
- Friendship Arch (➤ 56)
- Tours Mon–Fri 10, 3; Sun 11:15

These two museums off the National Mall are underattended, and more's the pity. Make the effort and you will find quiet galleries, wonderful collections of American art, and intelligent history.

History Two Smithsonian museums are housed in the 19th-century Greek-Revival Old Patent Office Building: the National Portrait Gallery and the National Museum of American Art.

National Portrait Gallery In the southern part of the building, the National Portrait Gallery superbly blends history and art, providing a context for the intimate story told through the portrait sitters and their legacies. Here you will find the stories of prominent Colonial Americans, First Peoples, American artists, inventors, industrialists, educators, politicians, and civic and military leaders. Exhibitions include aspects of portrait painting and historical events.

George Washington *from the collection of the National Portrait Gallery*

National Museum of American Art Housed in the northern part of the building, this museum features American folk art galleries, portrayals of the American West, George Catlin's paintings of American Indians, American Impressionists, the Ash Can School painters and other noted American painters such as John Singer Sargent, Thomas Eakins, Mary Cassatt, Romaine Brooks, and pop artist Jasper Johns.

16

NATIONAL ARCHIVES

Americans have neither a monarchy nor state religion, but they do worship law. Nowhere is this worship more apparent than in the National Archives.

History Occupied in 1935, John Russell Pope's beaux-arts building serves as the repository for the government's valuable documents. At the last count it contained 3.2 billion textual documents, 1.6 million maps, 14.9 million photographs, and enough film and videotapes to encircle the globe many times.

What to see After passing through a metal detector, visitors proceed reverently toward a thronelike structure in a domed rotunda with Corinthian columns and arched pediment. Raised at the center of the structure are enshrined the Declaration of Independence, the Bill of Rights, and the Constitution, sealed in bronze helium-filled cases covered with green ultraviolet filters. If you wanted actually to read the Charters of Freedom, as they are called, forget it. The conservation techniques employed make reading impossible, as does the steady stream of visitors patiently waiting their turn to cast their gaze upon the written, but no longer read, work. At the end of each day, after all the visitors and researchers have gone home, the security staff lower the throne and the Charters within into a bomb-proof vault beneath the exhibition floor for safekeeping.

Also on exhibition are murals by Barry Faulkner entitled *The Declaration of Independence* and *The Constitution*. There is a changing exhibition space that shows material from the vast collections maintained by the Archives—everything from letters to photographs, to posters.

HIGHLIGHTS

- Charters of Freedom
- Magna Carta, on loan from Ross Perot
- Murals by Barry Faulkner
- Changing exhibition gallery

INFORMATION

- H5
- Constitution Avenue at 7th Street NW
- 202/501–5205
- Daily 10–5:30
- Archives
- Excellent
- Free
- Smithsonian Institution (➤ 36), U.S. Capitol (➤ 43), U.S. Botanic Gardens (➤ 42)
- Tours daily at 10:15 and 1:15 (reservations required)

17

NATIONAL GALLERY OF ART

HIGHLIGHTS

- East Wing
- Glass tetrahedrons in plaza
- *Knife Edge Mirror Two Pieces*, Henry Moore
- Alexander Calder's mobile, East Wing atrium
- *Mercury* surrounded by Tuscan marble columns
- *The Alba Madonna*, Raphael
- *Venus and Adonis*, Titian
- *Daniel in the Lion's Den*, Rubens
- *Woman Holding a Balance*, Vermeer
- *The Skater*, Gilbert Stuart
- Waterwall visible from plaza and concourse

INFORMATION

- H5
- Madison Drive between 3rd and 7th Streets NW
- 202/737–4215
- Mon–Sat 10–5; Sun 11–6
- Waterfall Cafeteria
- Archives
- Excellent
- Free
- U.S. Botanic Gardens (➤ 42), U.S. Capitol (➤ 43), National Air and Space Museum (➤ 41)
- Tours daily

Young Washingtonians may be forgiven for feeling an overwhelming sense of civic pride when they realize that every American citizen owns an equal share of the acres of fine art to which they are exposed in the National Gallery of Art.

History When Andrew Mellon was secretary of the treasury (1921–1932), he realized that the capital city lacked a great gallery to show the development of Western art. He determined to remedy this failing and when he died in 1937 he left an endowment, his renowned collection of paintings and sculpture, to the American people and his dream to his son, Paul. Paul Mellon oversaw the construction of John Russell Pope's Classical-Revival building (opened in 1941) and, eventually, I.M. Pei's visually stunning East Wing, to my mind the most beautiful modern building in America, opened in 1978.

What to see The permanent collection begins with Italian Renaissance painting, including the Spanish painters Velasquez, El Greco, and Goya as well as Flemish, German, and Dutch painting from van der Weyden and Dürer to Rubens and Vermeer. The French are abundantly represented by Watteau, Corot, Manet, Renoir, and all the Pre-, Neo- and Post-Impressionists. Works by William Hogarth begin the tour of British painting that follows, from Gainsborough to Turner. The Americans, too, are widely represented by Gilbert Stuart, Winslow Homer, James McNeill Whistler, and many, many other contributors to the creative patrimony.

This preeminent museum also offers films, symposia, and lectures on the collection, while the "micro gallery" computerized collection brings the gallery right into the Information Age.

18

National Air & Space Museum

Why is the National Air and Space Museum the most visited museum in the world? Imagination. This museum allows parents and children alike to extend to the edges of imagination.

History This museum was the Smithsonian's bicentennial gift to the nation, opening in 1976. It houses a collection begun as early as 1861, when the first secretary of the Smithsonian encouraged experiments in balloon flight. Today the collection includes the Wright Brothers' 1903 *Flyer*; Charles Lindbergh's *Spirit of St. Louis*; Chuck Yeager's *Bell X-1*, in which he broke the sound barrier; and *The Voyager*, in which Dick Rutan and Jeana Yeager flew non-stop around the world.

What to see In the Space Halls stand the Columbia Space Shuttle, Apollo-Soyuz spacecraft, Skylab, and Lunar Exploration Vehicles, to name but a few of the spectacular rockets, missiles, and space vehicles on view. Also here, and at the center of ongoing controversy over the events leading to the end of World War II, is the *Enola Gay*, the plane that carried the atomic bomb dropped on Hiroshima, Japan.

HIGHLIGHTS

- Wright Brothers' 1903 *Flyer*
- Charles Lindbergh's *Spirit of St. Louis*
- Chuck Yeager's *Bell X-1 Glamorous Glennis*
- John Glenn's *Friendship* and *Apollo 11*
- Soviet "Sputnik"
- Vertical Flight Gallery
- Lunar Exploration Vehicles
- Amelia Earhart's Lockheed Vega 5B

INFORMATION

- H5
- Independence Avenue at 6th Street SW
- 202/357–2700
- Daily 10–5:30
- Wright Place, cafeteria
- L'Enfant Plaza
- Excellent
- Free
- U.S. Botanic Gardens (➤ 42), National Gallery of Art (➤ 40)

Spirit of St. Louis, *flown by Charles Lindbergh*

19

U.S. Botanic Gardens

HIGHLIGHTS

- Seasonal displays
- Cactus House
- Orchids and tropical plants
- Coffee, chocolate, and banyan trees
- Bartholdi Fountain

INFORMATION

- H5
- 1st Street SW and Maryland Ave
- 202/225–7099
- Daily 9–5
- Federal Center SW
- Excellent
- Free
- Smithsonian Institution (➤ 36), U.S. Capitol (➤ 43)

The poinsettia display at the U.S. Botanic Gardens in December is an annual take-in for many Washington families. If you visit during a weekday winter morning, when you may well be alone in the desert display, you can easily imagine a strong sun and a dry breeze.

History U.S. explorers needed a place to conserve the specimens they brought home from the South Seas, and Congress authorized the first greenhouse in 1842. The present 40,000-square-foot conservatory, an attractive combination of iron-and-glass greenhouse and stone orangeries, was erected in 1931 at the southwestern corner of Capitol Hill.

What to see The entrance hall serves as a seasonal gallery where the visitor may encounter Christmas poinsettias, spring tulips and hyacinths, or autumn chrysanthemums. Orchids are always on display. There is a permanent planting of high desert flora, as well as a steamy tropical exhibit.

Experienced citygoers, with the ability to ignore traffic whizzing by, appreciate the tiny pocket park across Independence Avenue, arguably the most beautiful in the city. The plantings frame and showcase the cast-iron Bartholdi Fountain, embellished with sea nymphs, monsters, tritons, and lighted globes, which dates from 1876. Frédéric-Auguste Bartholdi is best known as the sculptor of the Statue of Liberty, a gift from the French to the people of America. He designed this fountain for the Philadelphia Centennial Exhibition, intending it to represent the elements of light and water. Picnics can be held at the tables on the Summer Terrace.

20

U.S. CAPITOL

The dome of the U.S. Capitol is a familiar backdrop for television newscasters and politicians attempting to associate their pronouncements with this unrivaled symbol of American democracy.

History The dome was an engineering feat when undertaken in 1851 by Capitol architect Charles Walter and U.S. Army Quartermaster General Montgomery Meigs. It became a political symbol before it was half finished; Civil War broke out, and the Capitol housed the wounded and their caregivers. Many advised President Lincoln to halt construction, as happened to government projects such as the Washington Monument, but he was adamant that work on the dome continue as "a sign we intend the Union shall go on." The 9-million-pound, cast-iron dome rises 280 feet.

What to see Visitors first encounter the Great Rotunda created by the dome. You may wait here for a guide or wander freely alone in the public spaces. The large paintings hanging overhead, depicting scenes of George Washington's leadership, were painted from life and memory by his aide, John Trumbull. *The Apotheosis of Washington*, a fresco by Italian immigrant Constantino Brumidi, fills the ceiling with classical deities and the Founding Fathers. Brumidi, it was said at the time, consorted with "ladies of the night," whose likenesses then appeared as ample maidens ministering to George Washington at the very pinnacle of American power: the Capitol dome.

HIGHLIGHTS

- Rotunda
- Frescoes by Constantino Brumidi
- 10-ton bronze Columbus Doors
- Statuary Hall
- Old Senate Chamber

INFORMATION

- J5
- 1st Street between Independence and Constitution Avenues
- 202/225–6827
- Daily 9–3:45
- Capitol Cafeteria, Dining Room
- Capitol South
- Excellent
- Free
- Union Station (➤ 44), U.S. Botanic Gardens(➤ 42), Library of Congress (➤ 46), U.S. Supreme Court Building (➤ 45)
- Tours daily, every 15 mins. A pass to observe a session of Congress can be obtained from a senator's or representative's office by U.S. nationals. Foreign visitors apply at the ground-floor appointment desk. When Congress works overtime, the exterior dome light in the cupola is lit, and visitors are welcome on a first come, first served basis.

The dome's colonnade

21

UNION STATION

HIGHLIGHTS

- Main Hall
- Statues of Roman legionnaires
- East Hall
- Presidential Waiting Room
- Columbus Plaza

INFORMATION

- J4
- 40 Massachusetts Avenue NE
- 202/371–9441
- 24 hours for train service; stores, restaurants, and theaters vary
- Many, for all budgets
- Union Station
- Excellent
- Free
- U.S. Capitol and Capitol Hill attractions (► 43)

Union Station is a public treasure for all people: moviegoing teenagers, professional women shopping at lunch, dining deal-makers, commuting bureaucrats, and tourists taking in the sights.

History Architect Daniel H. Burnham lived up to his motto Make No Little Plans when he undertook the consolidation of the District's several train lines early this century. Burnham's *beaux-arts*, white-marble, vaulted Union Station was the largest train station in the world when it opened in 1907.

Completely renovated and reopened in 1988, today's Union Station includes restaurants for every budget, nine movie screens, and sophisticated boutique shopping, as well as serving as an active train terminal and Metro stop.

What to see The exterior allegorical neoclassical sculptures of fire, electricity, and mechanics set off the skyline, and a grand memorial to Christopher Columbus by Lorado Taft fronts the massive Doric colonnade.

Travelers by the thousand pass under the cavernous 96-foot-high coffered, gold-leaf embellished ceiling, guarded patiently by 46 statues of Roman legionnaires by sculptor Augustus Saint-Gaudens. The original Presidential Waiting Room is now a restaurant.

When you walk outside, to the right you can visit another recently restored Burnham building: the Old Post Office, which now houses the Smithsonian Postal Museum. And to the left, you can see contemporary *beaux-arts* styling in the new Thurgood Marshall Federal Judicial Center by Edward Larrabee Barnes.

22

U.S. SUPREME COURT BUILDING

One of the justices called this 1935 neo-classical gleaming Vermont marble building, designed by Cass Gilbert, Jr., "bombastically pretentious . . . for a quiet group of old boys such as the Supreme Court."

History Well, the Court is no longer an old boys' ghetto, with Justices Sandra Day O'Conner and Ruth Bader Ginsburg, and, in fact, it has never been really quiet. The 1857 *Dred Scott* decision, which held that Congress had no authority to limit slavery, contributed to the onset of the Civil War. Rulings on abortion have frequently made the wide, open court plaza a focus of civil disobedience. *Brown v. Board of Education* required the integration of schools and busing across the land, and *Engel v. Vitale* outlawed school prayer.

But, in another way, the Court does work quietly. The justices are appointed for life and rarely give interviews. The Court is not televised, and, unlike the rest of Washington, leaks of information never percolate out of this staid edifice.

What to see When the Court is in session (Oct–Jun), casual visitors can spend a few minutes viewing the workings of the Court by waiting in the "three-minute line." There is a small exhibition on Court history, and the building itself, one of Washington's most impressive Greek temples, is certainly worth the time. The magnificent bronze entrance doors, designed by John Donnely, Jr., and weighing 13 tons, depict the world's legal systems. Inside, sculpted friezes by James Earle Frazier show *The Contemplation of Justice* and *The Authority of Law.*

HIGHLIGHTS

- Bronze entrance doors
- Plaza sculpture
- Busts of chief justices
- Film and exhibits on Court history
- Statue of Justice John Marshall
- The Court in session

INFORMATION

- J5
- 1st and East Capitol Streets NE
- 202/479–3211
- Mon–Fri 9–4:30
- Cafeteria
- Capitol South, Union Station
- Excellent
- Free
- Library of Congress (➤ 46), U.S. Capitol (➤ 43)
- Lectures on the half-hour when the Court is not in session

Spring blossom softens the stern façade

23

LIBRARY OF CONGRESS

HIGHLIGHTS

- Neptune Fountain by Roland Hinton Perry
- "Torch of Learning" on green copper dome
- Great Hall
- Main Reading Room
- Stained glass, arched windows
- Sculpture inside and out
- View of the Capitol from the Madison Building cafeteria

INFORMATION

- J5
- 1st Street and Independence Avenue SE
- 202/707–5458
- Mon–Fri 8:30AM–9:30PM; Sat 8:30–6
- Cafeteria
- Capitol South
- Excellent. Visitor Services (202/707–9779) provides American Sign Language interpretation. TTY 202/707–6362
- Free
- U.S. Capitol (► 43), U.S. Supreme Court Building (► 45)
- Tours begin at the Jefferson Building Mon–Sat 11, 1, 2:30, 4:00

Library resources are open to any individual 18 years or older pursuing research

When asked about the advantages of living in Washington, many residents list the libraries. Chief among them is the Library of Congress.

History As early as 1800, Congress appropriated funds for a library. Unfortunately, when the British sacked the Capitol in 1814, they destroyed the library. Thomas Jefferson's personal library then became the nucleus of the new collection. The granite *beaux-arts* Jefferson Building is imposing, with a ceremonial portico, carved balustrades, Corinthian columns, massive quoins, and sculpted busts of men of letters gazing down on the passing scene. The Main Reading Room serves as a scholarly mecca. Sitting at the mahogany readers' tables 160 feet below the domed ceiling is an experience of an almost spiritual nature for many researchers.

What to see Today, more than 100 million items fill 600 miles of shelves in the Jefferson, Madison, and Adams buildings, clustered between 1st and 3rd Streets on Pennsylvania Avenue SE. Holdings include the largest map collection in the world, Jefferson's first version of the Declaration of Independence, a Gutenberg Bible, Lincoln's drafts of the Emancipation Proclamation and the Gettysburg Address, Stradivarius violins, the various contents of Lincoln's pockets on the evening he was shot, original scores by both Brahms and Beethoven, and props and papers belonging to Harry Houdini.

The copper dome and Torch of Learning

24

SHRINE OF THE IMMACULATE CONCEPTION

Big, ordered, crisp—these are some of the adjectives used to describe the National Shrine of the Immaculate Conception, dedicated to Christ's mother, Mary, named Patroness of the United States by Pope Pius IX in 1847.

History Work began in the grounds of Catholic University in 1920. In 1926 the Crypt Church was complete. After the Great Depression and World War II, construction began again in earnest during 1954. Having been completed with characteristic American efficiency, the Great Upper Church was dedicated on November 20, 1959.

What to see Separating the Crypt Church from the Chapel of Our Lady of Hostyn is a supremely delicate stained-glass screen depicting scenes from the life of Saint John Neumann, the first American man to have been canonized.

The Byzantine-style dome (237 feet in height and 108 feet in diameter) is lavishly decorated with Marian symbols in gold-leaf and colored tiles. The 329-foot-high bell tower houses a 56-bell carillon cast in France and supports a 20-foot gilded cross visible for miles around in every direction.

Three rose windows embellished with gold and amethyst illuminate the sanctuary, along with ranks of other windows depicting the lives of Mary, the Holy Family, saints, and redeemed sinners. But the lasting image visitors take away is that of the extraordinary mosaics, acres of them on ceilings and walls, in the apse and in chapels, donated by American Catholics of all ethnic origins.

HIGHLIGHTS

- Ecclesiastical sculpture
- Mosaics

INFORMATION

- Off map, north of K1
- 4th Street and Michigan Avenue NE
- 202/526–8300
- Apr–Oct 7–7. Nov–Mar 7–6
- Cafeteria daily 7:30–2:30
- Brookland
- Excellent
- Free
- Tours by appointment, Mon–Sat 9–12, 1–3; Sun 1:30–3

The Byzantine-style Christ in the dome

25

CEDAR HILL

HIGHLIGHTS

- Harriet Beecher Stowe's desk
- Rocking chair, gift of Republic of Haiti
- 1,000-volume library
- Portraits of Elizabeth Cady Stanton and Susan B. Anthony
- View of Washington

INFORMATION

L8
1411 W Street SE
202/426–5961
Daily: summer 9–5; winter 9-4. Closed Dec 25, Jan 1
By Tourmobile 202/554–7950
By car 11th Street Bridge to Martin Luther King Avenue, left on W Street
Good
Free
Hourly tours. Reservation 800/365–2267

Statue of Frederick Douglass

When historic houses hold the decorative arts, libraries and family mementos of the previous occupants, they can provide the intimacy of a personal visit. Cedar Hill, home of America's famous abolitionist Frederick Douglass, is such a place.

History Douglass, christened Frederick Augustus Washington Bailey about 1818, wrote that when his mother died seven years later, he had never seen her in daylight. He had been separated from her at birth by a distance of 12 miles, a distance she infrequently walked after work, leaving a few hours later to be back in the fields by sun up. Despite this humble beginning, Douglass learned the ship-caulker's trade, escaped to Paris to avoid slave bounty hunters, lectured widely and published on antislavery, became an adviser to President Lincoln, an ambassador to Haiti, and a staunch supporter of women's suffrage. When he moved into the Italianate-style Cedar Hill, he was the first black resident of Anacostia, breaking the prohibition against "Irish, Negro, mulatto, or persons of African blood."

What to see Cedar Hill, now the Frederick Douglass National Historic Site, occupies the highest point in Anacostia, with a great view of the Anacostia River and the capital city. The property is now operated by the National Park Service, which provides an information center and a bookstore specializing in African-American titles.

Among the many artifacts on display inside the house are the desk at which Harriet Beecher Stowe wrote *Uncle Tom's Cabin* and the 1,000 volumes that made up Frederick Douglass's original library.

WASHINGTON's *best*

AFRICAN-AMERICAN SITES

1212 T Street NW, the house where "Duke" Ellington grew up in the early 1900s

Lincoln Theater

Opened in 1922 as a first-run movie theater that catered to black patrons who were either barred from white theaters or forced to sit in the balcony, the theater has been restored to its original condition and now serves for performances of all kinds, contributing to the rejuvenation of the U Street corridor, once widely known as "Black Broadway."

G2 1215 U Street NW 202/328–6000 Open for performances U Street–Cardozo

See Top 25 Sights for
CEDAR HILL (► 48)
LINCOLN MEMORIAL (► 26)

ANACOSTIA MUSEUM

This Smithsonian museum depicts African-American art and heritage through changing exhibitions and public programs that attract neighborhood residents and visitors from the four corners of the globe.

M9 1901 Fort Place SE 202/287–3369 Daily 10–5 Call for shuttle schedule Free

EDWARD KENNEDY "DUKE" ELLINGTON RESIDENCE

Though born at 1217 22nd Street NW, Duke Ellington (1899–1974, ► 12) grew up on this street, taking piano lessons near by. He first appeared with his band, Duke's Serenaders, at True Reformers Hall, a local dance spot on U Street. By 1931, he was being described as "the biggest inspiration we had … the epitome of what we wanted to be," following his performance at the gala reopening of the Howard Theater.

G2 1212 T Street NW Not open to the public U Street–Cardozo

FATHER PATRICK FRANCIS HEALY BUILDING, GEORGETOWN UNIVERSITY

This 1879 baronial fantasy dominating Georgetown University's Potomac riverfront honors the first black Catholic priest and bishop in America, who later became president of Georgetown University.

C3 37th and O Streets NW 202/687–5055 24 hours

FREDERICK DOUGLASS HOUSE

This Victorian townhouse was the first Washington home of one of the country's most famous abolitionists. It later housed the National Museum of African Art, now part of the Smithsonian museums.

K5 316 A Street NE Not open to the public Capitol South

HOWARD UNIVERSITY

Chartered in 1867 to educate freed men and women, Howard's neocolonial, neo-Georgian and modern buildings on 89 acres today house 12,000 students pursuing nearly 200 areas of study. Howard Law School is widely acknowledged as the place where African-Americans learned the legal system that they later used to drive the civil rights movement of the 1960s. Thurgood Marshall, associate justice of the Supreme Court, was a Howard graduate.

H2 2400 6th Street NW 20059 202/806–6100 Mon–Fri 9–5 Shaw–Howard University

INDUSTRIAL BANK OF WASHINGTON
Blacks could deposit money in white banks, but the banks would not lend to black homeowners or entrepreneurs. When John L. Lewis opened his bank here in 1913, it soon became known as "the wage earners' bank." In 1932 Texan Jesse Mitchell opened Industrial on this site with $200,000; the bank still serves Washington's African-American community.
G2 2000 11th Street NW 202/722–2050 Mon–Fri 9–3; Fri 4:30–6; Sat 9–noon U Street–Cardozo

LINCOLN PARK
Charlotte Scott, a Virginian woman, contributed the first $5 toward the Emancipation Memorial, which was supported entirely from funds from free blacks. Dedicated on April 14, 1876, it remained the city's only monument to Lincoln until 1922 when the Lincoln Memorial was dedicated. In 1974, the Emancipation Memorial was turned away from the Capitol, toward the new memorial to Mary McLeod Bethune (► 12).
K5 East Capitol Street between 11th and 13th Streets
Eastern Market

TRUE REFORMERS HALL
This six-story 1903 building housed a variety of black-owned retail stores, entertainments, offices, and a drill room and armory for Washington's black National Guard unit. The United Order of True Reformers awarded architect John A. Lankford his first major commission with this building. The building later housed a popular dance hall, where "Duke" Ellington performed (► 12 and 50), and the Metropolitan Police Boys Club for black children.
G2 1200 U Street NW U Street–Cardozo

Black Broadway

Since the 1968 riots sparked by the assassination of Martin Luther King, Jr., U Street NW, near the U Street–Cardozo Metro, has undergone a transformation. With the reopening in 1994 of the 1,250-seat Lincoln Theater, the strip once again deserves the appellation "Black Broadway." *Community Rhythms*, the vibrant murals of artist Al Smith, decorate the Metro entrances and depict the area's renaissance.

Mary McLeod Bethune Memorial, Lincoln Park

MARY McLEOD BETHUNE
1875 1955
Let her works praise her

For Children

Information Sources

The Washington Post "Carousel Weekend" lists up-to-the-moment events for children. WKDL radio (1050 AM) caters to children and their parents and often reports on children's events.

The National Museum of American History

See Top 25 Sights for
BUREAU OF ENGRAVING AND PRINTING (➤ 35)
FBI BUILDING (➤ 37)
NATIONAL GEOGRAPHIC SOCIETY, EXPLORERS HALL (➤ 29)
UNION STATION (➤ 44)

THE SMITHSONIAN MUSEUMS

These museums entertain and educate millions of children every year about everything from aardvarks and airplanes to singing insects and space suits. Of special interest are the dinosaurs and the insect zoo at the National Museum of Natural History (G5 Constitution Avenue and 12th Street NW); the Hands-on-History and Hands-on-Science rooms at the National Museum of American History (➤ 34); "Amazonia" and the Invertebrate House at the National Zoological Park (➤ 53); the IMAX films at the National Air and Space Museum (➤ 41); and Discovery Theater (G5 900 Jefferson Drive SW 202/357–1500), where puppet shows, plays, and storytelling are held. 202/357–2700.

CAPITAL CHILDREN'S MUSEUM

Everything is messy here, as if a horde of happy children had played with everything for years, and they have. Permanent exhibitions explore Mexican and Thai cultures, animation, drawing from life and children's art, and children's health and well-being.
J4 800 3rd Street NE 202/675–4120 Daily 10–5
6 Union Station Inexpensive

HARD ROCK CAFÉ

A restaurant and a worldwide happening, complete with T-shirts and baseball caps. Kids and their parents love the up-beat rock and roll hall of fame atmosphere and good-sized portions.
G4 999 E Street NW 202/737–7625 Weekdays 11–midnight; weekends 11AM–1AM Metro Center

METRO

Kids love the underground Metro system. Parents should be aware that Washingtonians use the escalators as urban exercise machines, so stand right, walk left. No eating, drinking, or smoking in the Metro.

NATIONAL AQUARIUM

Opened in 1873, the aquarium attracts youngsters with a popular touch-tank, sea turtles, moray eels, and tropical and freshwater fish. Shark and piranha feedings take place at 2 o'clock on alternate days.
G5 14th Street and Pennsylvania Avenue NW
202/482–2825 Daily 9–5 Federal Triangle
Inexpensive

NATIONAL ZOOLOGICAL PARK

Within the 160 acres landscaped by Frederick Law Olmsted, Sr., in 1889, zoo designers have constantly renovated enclosures to provide natural settings for birds, hoofed stock, komodo dragons, pygmy hippopotamuses, big cats, monkeys, and much more. The Invertebrate House provides quiet for children to enjoy rarely seen animals.

E1 3001 Connecticut Avenue NW 202/673–4717 Grounds: 15 Apr–15 Oct 8–8; 16 Oct–14 Apr, 8–6. Animal Buildings: 9–4:30. "Amazonia": 10–4 Snack bars Woodley Park–Zoo Free

NAVY MUSEUM

Big, showy ships, cannons, missiles, and submarines provide plenty of opportunities to peer through periscopes and pretend to conquer the seven seas.

K7 9th and M Streets SE, Building 76 202/433–4882 Weekdays 9–4; weekends and holidays 10–5 Eastern Market, Navy Yard Free

PLANET HOLLYWOOD

Owned by movie stars, including Sylvester Stallone and Bruce Willis, and decorated with cinema memorabilia, this restaurant specializes in burgers, pizzas, pasta, and other American favorites. A merchandizing arm sells everything from caps to jackets.

G5 1101 Pennsylvania Avenue NW 202/783–7827 Daily 11AM–midnight Federal Triangle

PUPPET COMPANY PLAYHOUSE

Located in Glen Echo Park, MD, this troupe presents plays beloved by children of all ages.

Off map 7300 MacArthur Boulevard, Glen Echo, MD 301/320–6668 Free annual puppet exhibition; tickets cheap

SHOPPING FOR KIDS

FAO Schwarz stocks the best (or at least the most expensive) toys, dolls, children's books, and much more.

D3 3222 M Street NW 202/342–2285 Mon–Sat 10–9; Sun 11–6 Café

The Kid's Closet sells baby clothes and gifts.

F3 1226 Connecticut Avenue NW 202/429–9247 Mon–Fri 10–6; Sat 11–5 Dupont Circle

WASHINGTON DOLLS' HOUSE AND TOY MUSEUM

This museum has an extensive collection of Victorian dolls, dollhouses, toys, and games.

Off map at D1 5236 44th Street NW 202/244–0024 Tue–Sat 10–5; Sun noon–5 Friendship Heights Inexpensive

Tigers and other endangered species are bred at Washington's National Zoological Park

Baby-sitters

For sitters, check with the hotel concierge or call

Chevy Chase Babysitters

10771 Middleboro Drive, Damascus, MD 20872

301/916–2694

Mothers' Aides Inc.

Box 7088, Fairfax Station, VA 22039 703/250–0700

WeeSit

10681 Oak Thrust Court, Burke, VA 22015

703/764–1542

LIBRARIES & ARCHIVES

See Top 25 Sights for
LIBRARY OF CONGRESS (► 46)
NATIONAL ARCHIVES (► 39)

National Council of Negro Women

The Mary McLeod Bethune Museum and Archives house the records of the National Council of Negro Women, founded in 1935 and uniting the considerable influence of hundreds of African-American women's groups. These women shaped public policy regarding civil rights, health care, housing, and employment, extending even to the formation of the United Nations.

BETHUNE MUSEUM AND ARCHIVES

Located in a Victorian townhouse near historic Logan Circle, this site is dedicated to preserving and documenting black women's participation in American history. Mary McLeod Bethune, political activist, educator, and founder of the National Council of Negro Women, lived in this house, which also served as the headquarters of the Council.

➕ G3 ✉ 1318 Vermont Avenue NW ☎ 202/332–1233 🕓 Sep–May Mon–Fri 10–4. Jun–Aug Mon–Sat 10–4 🚇 U Street–Cardozo, McPherson Square

FOLGER SHAKESPEARE LIBRARY

The world's most comprehensive collection of Shakespeare's works is included in this collection of 275,000 books and manuscripts from and about the European Renaissance. Collections are made available to scholars by appointment.

➕ J5 ✉ 201 E Capitol, SE ☎ 202/544–4600 🕓 Open to researchers Mon–Fri 10–4 🚇 Capitol South

HISTORICAL SOCIETY OF WASHINGTON

Here are text and image collections related to the social history of the District of Columbia. The society is located in the ornate Victorian Heurich Mansion, built by a wealthy brewer.

➕ F3 ✉ 1307 New Hampshire Avenue NW ☎ 202/785–2068 🕓 Wed–Sat noon–4 🚇 Dupont Circle 💷 Cheap

MARTIN LUTHER KING MEMORIAL LIBRARY

The large, active, urban, main branch of the D.C. public library system, M.L.K. has an extensive Washingtoniana collection, as well as a Black Studies Division. Mies van der Rohe designed this unadorned steel-and-glass building, which opened in 1972 and is softened by Don Miller's mural celebrating the life of Martin Luther King, Jr.

➕ G4 ✉ 901 G Street NW ☎ 202/727–1111 🕓 Mon–Thu 10–7; Fri–Sat 10–5:30 🚇 Gallery Place

MOORLAND-SPINGARN RESEARCH CENTER

The Center includes extensive archives and secondary material about the African diaspora. Researchers are welcome in this noncirculating library.

➕ H2 ✉ 500 Howard Place in Founders Library, Howard University ☎ 202/806–7239 🕓 Mon–Fri 9–4:45 🚇 Shaw–Howard University

NATIONAL GEOGRAPHIC SOCIETY LIBRARY

This little-known library houses 50,000 books on geography, natural history, travel, and topics that have

long interested the Society, such as polar exploration. Of course, all the Society's publications, including a complete run of the famous yellow-spined magazine begun in 1888, are available. The reading room is well appointed with an automated catalog, good light, and warm wood paneling.
F3 17th and M Streets NW 202/857–7783 By appointment Dupont Circle, Farragut North

SMITHSONIAN INSTITUTION LIBRARIES
Smithsonian museums all have libraries open by appointment to researchers, from schoolchildren to scholars. Collections include images of airplanes of all periods, worldwide biological flora and fauna, space, film and television, linguistics, paleobiology, the history of railroads, women's political life, domestic industry, war, peace, and everything in between. Of special note are the Archives of American Art, the National Anthropological Archives, and the Human Studies Film Archives (► 36).
202/357–1300

SUMNER SCHOOL MUSEUM AND ARCHIVES
Architect Adolph Cluss won a Medal for Progress at the Vienna World's Exposition in 1873 for his innovative use of hallways and closets to shield classrooms from exterior noise. The school stood as a model example of black education during segregation It now houses the archives of the D.C. Public Schools.
F3 17th and M Streets NW 202/727–3419 Tue–Fri 10–5 Dupont Circle

A bookworm's paradise

When listing the reasons to live inside the Capital Beltway, many Washingtonians praise the literary scene. Museums and historic sites have acres of bookshelves, crammed with publications related to the museum collection and historic events, and most have libraries open to researchers. Throughout the city, specialized collections are open to scholars and students of everything from Jewish-American military history to Shakespeare.

Exhibits at the National Geographic Society

OUTDOOR SPACES

GARDENS, SCULPTURE, & MEN ON HORSES

Washington summers can be sticky, but do not let the heat deter you from an exploration of the often inspiring, often whimsical sculptural placements, many of which are in lovely gardens with plenty of shade.

Friendship Arch

Located at the Chinatown Metro, this gilded arch symbolizes the energy and vitality of Washington's Asian community.

H4 Chinatown, 7th and G Streets NW 24 hours Gallery Place–Chinatown Free

See Top 25 Sights for
BARTHOLDI FOUNTAIN AT THE U.S. BOTANIC GARDENS (➤ 42)
COLUMBUS PLAZA AT UNION STATION (➤ 44)
JEFFERSON MEMORIAL (➤ 32)
LINCOLN MEMORIAL (➤ 26)
NEPTUNE'S COURT AT THE LIBRARY OF CONGRESS (➤ 46)
VIETNAM VETERANS MEMORIAL AND CONSTITUTION GARDENS (➤ 28)
WASHINGTON MONUMENT (➤ 31)

THE AWAKENING

The Awakening, by J. Seward Johnson, was installed as part of a temporary outdoor exhibition. So many Washingtonians, especially children, appreciated the bearded aluminum giant rising from the tip of Hains Point that it was retained. The park in which it is set offers jogging and bike paths, tennis, swimming, flowering cherry trees, and a golf driving range.

H9 Hains Point, East Potomac Park 202/485–9880, 202/727–6523 24 hours Free

BISHOPS GARDEN

In total, there are 57 acres at Washington National Cathedral, tended by the All Hallows Guild, which hosts an annual flower show to raise funds for the gardens. The jewel in this crown is the Bishops Garden, which is designed around European ruins and a statue of the Prodigal Son. Plantings include herbs, boxwood, magnolia trees, and tea roses.

C1/D1 Wisconsin and Massachusetts Avenues NW 202/537–6200 May–Labor Day Mon–Fri 10–9; Sat and Sun 10–4:30. Labor Day–30 April daily 10–4:30 Tenley Town; 30 series bus south Free

DUMBARTON OAKS

In 1944 the international conference leading to the formation of the United Nations was held at this estate, also known for its fine 10-acre formal garden.

D2 31st and R Streets NW 202/339–6400 Daily 2–5 Cheap

EINSTEIN MEMORIAL

Nestled in the grounds of one of Washington's most staid and august organizations, the National Academy of Sciences, is Robert Berks's whimsical

sculpture of the physicist Albert Einstein, gently feeding the birds and inviting generations of children to sit on his lap.
E5 22nd Street NW and Constitution Avenue, in the grounds of the National Academy of Sciences 24 hours Foggy Bottom Free

FDR MEMORIAL
Ten bronze sculptures depict Franklin Delano and Eleanor Roosevelt, and events from the Great Depression and World War II. The park includes waterfalls and FDR's inspiring words carved in red Dakota granite. Dedicated in 1997, the memorial is near the Lincoln, Vietnam and Korean War Memorials.
F6 West Potomac Park 202/228–2491 Daylight hours half-hour walk from Smithsonian Free

GRANT MEMORIAL
General Ulysses S. Grant looks somewhat weary from the weight of his struggles as he sits on horseback at the foot of Capitol Hill. Animated artillery and cavalry flank Grant and create the city's most effective sculptural group of men on horses.
H5 1st Street NW at the foot of Capitol Hill 24 hours Capitol South Free

HIRSHHORN SCULPTURE GARDEN
For a respite from the cultural intensity of the National Mall, why not stop at this walled, sunken garden, where you will be surrounded by works by such luminaries as Henry Moore, Max Ernst, Pablo Picasso, and Man Ray?
H5 7th Street and Jefferson Drive SW 202/357–2700 7:30AM–dusk L'Enfant Plaza Free

NATIONAL ARBORETUM
The Arboretum's 444 acres invite driving, biking, hiking, and even roller-blading. The Herbarium maintains 500,000 dried plants for research purposes, the azalea walk is a spring favorite, and the National Herb Garden and National Bonsai Collection are both meccas for serious gardeners and general visitors alike.
M3/N3 3501 New York Avenue NE 202/245–2726 Daily 8–5 Free

ROCK CREEK PARK
Washingtonians enjoy 1,800-acre Rock Creek Park as a contrast to the concrete, asphalt, and marble found everywhere else in the city. Picnicking, biking, hiking, tennis, golf, and riding may all be enjoyed. The Nature Center and Planetarium have a full year-round schedule.
E1/E2/E3 Nature Center, 5000 Glover Road NW 202/426–6829 Nature Center: Wed–Sun 9–5. Grounds: daylight hours Woodley Park–Zoo Free

Grant Memorial below Capitol Hill

Korean War Veterans Memorial

Dedicated in 1995, this memorial includes 19 life-size figures marching up an incline toward the American flag, a still pool memorializing those who lost their lives in the war, and photographs of the Korean conflict etched into a 60-foot wall. This memorial of faces serves as a compelling counterpoint to the wall of names of the Vietnam Veterans Memorial.
E5 Between the Lincoln Memorial and Independence Avenue 202/208–3561 24 hours Free

Places of Worship

Washington Jewish Week

Washington Catholics have the National Shrine of the Immaculate Conception; Episcopalians have the National Cathedral; and Jewish citizens look to the *Washington Jewish Week*, available at most newsstands, to keep abreast of area events and local Jewish life.

Minaret of the Islamic Mosque and Cultural Center

See Top 25 Sights for
U.S. HOLOCAUST MEMORIAL MUSEUM (➤ 33)
SHRINE OF THE IMMACULATE CONCEPTION (➤ 47)

ADAS ISRAEL CONGREGATION

Conservative congregation.
2850 Quebec Street NW 202/362–4433
Cleveland Park

BET MISH PACHAH SYNAGOGUE

Gay and lesbian congregation.
Box 141 202/833–1638 Services held at National City Christian Church 5 Thomas Circle NW

THE IMANI TEMPLE

American Catholic congregation, founded by Reverend Stalings.
K5 609–611 Maryland Avenue NE 202/388–8155
Daily 9–6 Union Station

ISLAMIC MOSQUE AND CULTURAL CENTER

Exclaiming its purpose, the 162-foot minaret calls the faithful five times daily into this center for all American Moslems. Inside, Arabic art includes Persian carpets, ebony and ivory carvings, stained glass, and mosaics.
E2 2551 Massachusetts Avenue NW 202/332–8343
Cultural Center: daily 10:30–4:30. For prayer: dawn–10:30PM
Dupont Circle

KESHER ISRAEL CONGREGATION

Orthodox congregation.
2801 N Street NW 202/333–4808 Foggy Bottom

METROPOLITAN AFRICAN METHODIST EPISCOPAL CHURCH

Completed in 1886, this redbrick Gothic Revival church, known as the national cathedral of the AME movement, was paid for by ex-slaves and built by African-American craftsmen and artisans.
G3 1518 M Street NW 202/331–1426 Mon–Sat 10–6 Home-cooked lunch Thu, Fri 11–2 Farragut North

MOUNT ZION HERITAGE CENTER AND METHODIST CHURCH

This congregation established in 1816 educated black children and adults, created the first black library in the District, operated a cemetery for African-Americans, and served as a stop on the Underground Railroad in the 19th century. The late 19th-century brick church is known for its elaborate pressed-tin ceiling, wood engravings by African artisans, and

embellished cast-iron pillars.
E3 1334 29th Street NW 202/234–0148 Easily arranged by appointment

ST. JOHN'S EPISCOPAL CHURCH
Built by Benjamin Latrobe in a Greek Cross form, the church has later additions, including the Doric portico and cupola tower. Pew 54 is reserved for the president, who has worshipped here since the church opened in 1816.
F4 1525 H Street NW 202/347–8766 Mon–Fri 8–4; Sat 9–3; Sun services 8, 9, 11 McPherson Square

ST. MARY'S EPISCOPAL CHURCH
James Renwick designed this redbrick 1887 Gothic Revival church for the first black Protestant Episcopal congregation in Washington. The building includes a timber roof and French painted-glass windows depicting St. Cyprian and other African religious leaders. A tiny garden offers moments of peace and quiet in the midst of the downtown bustle.
E4 728 23rd Street NW 202/333–3985 Daily 9–2 Foggy Bottom

ST. MATTHEW'S CATHEDRAL
President John F. Kennedy's funeral mass was held in this plain Renaissance-style church, the seat of Washington's Catholic archbishop. The embellished interior includes stunning mosaics and gilded Corinthian capitals.
F3 1725 Rhode Island Avenue NW 202/347–3215 Sun–Fri 7–6:30; Sat 8–7 Farragut North

WASHINGTON HEBREW CONGREGATION
Reformed congregation.
3935 Macomb Street NW 202/362–7100

WASHINGTON NATIONAL CATHEDRAL
On September 30, 1990, President George Bush and thousands of other guests watched the placement of the final stone of this inspiring Gothic-style building, resplendent with flying buttresses, 565-foot nave, rose window made up of 10,500 pieces of stained glass, stone barrel vaults, and fanciful gargoyles. The stone carving in this, the sixth-largest cathedral in the world, is quite extraordinary. Bring binoculars to inspect the details.
C1 Wisconsin and Massachusetts Avenues NW 202/537–6200 May–Labor Day Mon–Fri 10–9; Sat and Sun 10–4:30. Labor Day–30 Apr daily 10–4:30 Yes Tenley Town; 30 series bus south

Quiet places

Do not overlook the Hall of Remembrance in the U.S. Holocaust Memorial Museum. This space invites quiet, nondenominational contemplation, as does Barnett Newman's *14 Stations of the Cross* hanging on the concourse level of the National Gallery of Art.

Washington National Cathedral

VIEWS

Food with a view

For learning about the city, the clock tower at the Old Post Office has the best view, and the building houses a food court with everything from ice cream to Indian food. The tower bells, cast in London in 1976, were donated to Congress to commemorate the American Revolution.

See Top 25 Sights for
CEDAR HILL (➤ 48)
CUSTIS-LEE MANSION AT ARLINGTON NATIONAL CEMETERY (➤ 24)
KENNEDY CENTER ROOF TERRACE (➤ 25)
LIBRARY OF CONGRESS CAFETERIA (➤ 46)
U.S. CAPITOL, WEST FACE (➤ 43)
WASHINGTON MONUMENT (➤ 31)

HOTEL WASHINGTON ROOF TERRACE

This national landmark is the oldest continuously operating hotel in the city, known since its opening in 1918 as the hotel with the view. The terrace overlooks the White House and the Washington Monument and is *the* place for afternoon tea or sunset cocktails.
G4 515 15th Street NW 202/638–5900
14 Apr–30 Oct 11AM–1AM McPherson Square Expensive

OLD POST OFFICE BUILDING TOWER

The fanciful, granite "old tooth" clock tower stands out amid the neoclassical surroundings of the Federal Triangle. The elevator ride to the top allows a close-up view of the city's topography and architecture.
G5 Pennsylvania Avenue at 12th Street NW
202/606– 8691 Easter– Labor Day daily 8AM–11PM. Sep–Mar daily 10–6 Yes Federal Triangle Free

The view from the Old Post Office tower

WASHINGTON *where to...*

ITALIAN

Prices

Average three-course meal per head, excluding tax and tips

$$$ = over $35

$$ = $20–$35

$ = up to $20

All restaurants mentioned here take the major credit cards. It is usually advisable to make a telephone reservation.

Door-to-door dining

If you find yourself hungry in your room, but don't want room service food, try one of several pizza delivery services. Domino's is the largest chain, with many locations. Pizza Hut has a few delivery outlets. Armand's (☎ 202/547–6600 on Capitol Hill or 202/363 5500 for upper Wisconsin Avenue), Geppetto (☎ 202/333–4315, in Georgetown), and Trio Pizza (☎ 202/232–5611, near Dupont Circle), all deliver good pizzas.

BICE ($$)
This popular restaurant is known for its pastas and risottos, and offers duck served several ways: smoked, roasted, and in ravioli.
H5 ✉ 601 Pennsylvania Ave NW (entrance is on Indiana Ave) ☎ 202/638–2423 Closed Sat lunch and Sun Archives

GALILEO ($$$)
Known for its wine list, home-made items from breadsticks to mozzarella, and Italian specialties of grilled fish, game birds, and veal, Galileo changes its menu twice daily.
F4 ✉ 1110 21st Street NW ☎ 202/293–7191 Weekdays breakfast, lunch, and dinner; weekends dinner only Foggy Bottom

I MATTI ($$)
The less-expensive sister restaurant to Galileo, i Matti has an extensive menu ranging from pizza to homey polenta, with lots of daily dinner specials, such as rabbit cutlet.
F2 ✉ 2436 18th Street NW ☎ 202/462–8844 Mon–Sat lunch and dinner; Sun dinner only Woodley Park–Zoo

I RICCHI ($$$)
This airy Tuscan dining room, with terracotta tiles and floral frescoes, attracts the business crowd with spit-roasted meats and a seasonal menu.
F3 ✉ 1220 19th Street NW ☎ 202/835–0459 Closed Sat lunch and Sun Dupont Circle

IL RADICCHIO ($)
A young, funky crowd comes here for the all-you-can-eat spaghetti dinner, with a choice of 20 different toppings, and the neighborhood's café scene.
F3 ✉ 1509 17th Street NW ☎ 202/986–2627 Closed Sun lunch Dupont Circle

OTELLO ($)
Inexpensive, simply prepared meat and fish dishes, such as red snapper with capers and olives. Quaint.
F3 ✉ 1329 Connecticut Avenue NW ☎ 202/429–0209 Mon–Fri lunch and dinner; Sat dinner only. Closed Sun Dupont Circle

PIZZERIA PARADISO ($)
This pizzeria, with a trompe l'oeil ceiling, has fresh versions of the basics: pizzas, salads, and sandwiches.
F3 ✉ 2029 P Street NW ☎ 202/223–1245 Daily lunch and dinner Dupont Circle

PRIMI PIATTI ($$)
The house specialties here include pastas, antipasti and grilled items.
F4 ✉ 2013 I Street NW ☎ 202/223–3600 Closed Sat lunch and Sun Farragut West

TRATTORIA AL SOLE ($$$)
The accent is on seafood in this airy restaurant, part of which is in a glass-roofed courtyard.
F3 ✉ 1606 20th Street NW ☎ 202/667–0047 Closed Sat lunch and Sun Dupont Circle

French

BISTRO FRANCAIS ($$)
This French country restaurant offers good-value fixed-price lunches and early and late-night dinner specials and stays open until 3AM Sun–Thu, 4AM Fri and Sat.
D3 3128 M Street NW 202/338-3830 Daily lunch and dinner

CITRONELLE AT THE LATHAM HOTEL ($$$)
Consistently rated one of Washington's top restaurants, Citronelle serves contemporary, creative food.
D3 Latham Hotel, 3000 M Street NW 202/625-2150 Daily breakfast, lunch, and dinner There is no nearby Metro stop

GERARD'S PLACE ($$$)
Gerard Pangaud, the Washington area's only Michelin two-star chef, takes New American fare to new heights; try the seared tuna.
G4 915 15th Street NW 202/737-4445 Closed Sat lunch and Sun McPherson Square

LA BRASSERIE ($$)
The mostly French menu changes daily at this Capitol Hill townhouse restaurant. The crême brulée is reliably excellent. A spot for power-breakfasts.
J5 239 Massachusetts Avenue NE 202/546-9154 Daily breakfast, lunch, and dinner Union Station

LA CHAUMIERE ($$$)
With the rustic charm of a French country inn, this restaurant serves French provincial fare such as pot-au-feu and bouillabaisse.
E3 2813 M Street NW 202/338-1784 Closed Sat lunch and Sun

LA COLLINE ($$)
Seafood—fricassee, grilled or gratiné—is one measure of this consistently excellent yet reasonably priced Capitol Hill favorite.
J5 400 N Capitol Street NW 202/737-0400 Weekdays breakfast; closed Sat lunch and Sun Union Station

LA FOURCHETTE ($$)
This bit of Paris in Adams-Morgan, with tin ceiling, bentwood chairs, and quasi-Post-Impressionist murals, offers sturdy bistro cuisine, such as veal and lamb shanks.
F2 2429 18th Street NW 202/332-3077 Closed weekend lunch Woodley Park–Zoo (6 blocks)

LE LION D'OR ($$$)
Some say this was Washington's first national-class restaurant, where you'll find classic French cuisine in an old Continental-style room, complete with leather banquettes and tableside service wagons.
F3 1150 Connecticut Avenue NW (entrance on 18th Street NW) 202/296-7972 Mon–Sat dinner Farragut North

Quality dining

Long considered a city of mediocre restaurants, Washington in the last few years has come a long way in proving itself to be a city of quality dining. The city has the good fortune to have a chef who was given a two-star rating by the highly regarded *Guide Michelin*: Gerard Pangaud, of Gerard's Place.

Steak & Seafood

Seafood southwest

Washington is filled with restaurants of every imaginable ethnic variety. If you have a taste for fish, head down to the southwest waterfront, where there is a concentration of seafood restaurants. In Water Street you will find Phillips Flagship; Le Rivage (for French fish dishes); Hogates; Pier Seven; the Gangplank; and, for a Cajun twist, Creole Orleans.

GEORGETOWN SEAFOOD GRILL ($$)
This unpretentious Georgetown restaurant brings crabcakes, lobster, and softshell crabs to diners in wooden booths. At night, it features a raw bar.
D3 3063 M Street NW 202/333–7038 Daily lunch and dinner

LEGAL SEAFOOD ($$–$$$)
The Boston-based chain has arrived in Washington, offering up to 40 kinds of fish.
F4 2020 K Street NW 202/496–1111 Daily lunch and dinner Farragut West

LES HALLES ($$)
The beef here is American, but the preparation is strictly French. There is an upstairs area for cigar smoking.
G5 1201 Pennsylvania Avenue NW 202/347–6848 Daily lunch and dinner Federal Triangle

MORTON'S OF CHICAGO ($$$)
It's not the vinyl-boothed dining room that draws people here, it's the quantity as well as the quality of their steaks. If you're really hungry (or sharing), try the 3-pound porterhouse.
D3 3251 Prospect Street NW 202/342–6258 Dinner only

THE PALM ($$$)
Its plain decor is patterned after the New York original, and the business-like air is matched by the clientele. In addition to huge steaks, the Palm also offers a bargain lunch menu that includes shrimp, veal, and chicken salad.
F3 1225 19th Street NW 202/293–9091 Closed weekend lunch Dupont Circle

PESCE ($$)
Here you can dine on daily seafood specials like roasted monkfish, or buy fresh fish from the fish market.
F3 2016 P Street NW 202/466–FISH Mon–Sat lunch and dinner; Sun dinner only Dupont Circle

PRIME RIB ($$$)
Decorated in black and gold like a 1940s supper club, Prime Rib serves its namesake for the posh meat-and-potatoes set.
F4 2020 K Street NW 202/466–8811 Closed Sat lunch, Sun Farragut West

SAM AND HARRY'S ($$$)
Understated and genteel, this dining room packs them in with porterhouse and strip steaks, prime rib, and daily seafood specials.
F3 1200 19th Street NW 202/296–4333 Closed Sat lunch and Sun Dupont Circle

SEA CATCH ($$$)
This formal Georgetown establishment, hidden in a courtyard overlooking the C & O Canal, has an outstanding raw bar and well-prepared favorites like boiled lobster.
D3 1054 31st Street NW 202/337–8855 Closed Sun

NEW AMERICAN

CALIFORNIA PIZZA KITCHEN ($)
Bright, shiny, and mirrored, this busy restaurant does pizza and pasta the California way.
F3 1260 Connecticut Avenue NW 202/331–4020 Daily lunch and dinner Dupont Circle

CITIES ($$)
The front dining area and bar look like a service station. In the back dining room, every few months a different world capital is chosen as the theme, with decor and menu to match.
F2 2424 18th Street NW 202/328–7194 Dinner Mon–Sat No nearby Metro

KINKEAD'S ($–$$)
You can watch your meal being prepared in the open kitchen upstairs, which specializes in seafood offerings. The bar and café downstairs offer American-style tapas and other inexpensive fare.
F4 2000 Pennsylvania Avenue NW 202/296–7700 Daily lunch and dinner Foggy Bottom

NEW HEIGHTS ($$)
Attractively decorated to appeal to discreet celebrities. The frequently changed menu always has vegetarian options like Thai ravioli and expertly prepared grilled salmon.
E1 2317 Calvert Street NW 202/234–4110 Closed lunch Mon–Sat Woodley Park Zoo

NORA ($$)
The menu changes daily in this exposed-brick and quilt-decorated restaurant. Organic vegetables and free-range meats come in unusual combinations. Extensive dessert list.
E3 2132 Florida Avenue NW 202/462–5143 Closed lunch and Sun Dupont Circle

OCCIDENTAL GRILL ($$–$$$)
The photo-covered walls suggest an old Washington club, but while the patrons are loyal, the menu is less conservative, with grilled meats and marinated tuna.
G4 1475 Pennsylvania Avenue NW 202/783–1475 Daily lunch and dinner Metro Center

TABARD INN ($$)
With its parlorlike dining rooms and its lovely outdoor dining terrace, the Tabard serves its own organically grown vegetables (in season) and hormone-free beef.
F3 1739 N Street NW 202/833–2668 Daily breakfast, lunch, and dinner Dupont Circle

1789 ($$$)
Housed in a Federal town house with a large fireplace, 1789 specializes in game and seafood.
C3 1226 36th Street NW 202/965–1789 Daily dinner only

701 RESTAURANT ($$)
This very elegant restaurant, with large windows looking out on Pennsylvania Avenue, offers tapas, a caviar bar, and live jazz every night.
H5 701 Pennsylvania Avenue NW 202/393–0701 Closed weekend lunch Archives

Hotel restaurants

Some of Washington's best restaurants are in the finer hotels. Among them are Citronelle in the Latham Hotel (➤ 85), the Jefferson Hotel restaurant, the Morrison-Clark Inn (➤ 85), and Lafayette at the Hay-Adams Hotel (➤ 84). They all serve creative, contemporary fare, drawing on the best American ingredients and classic French cooking techniques. Though all tend toward the expensive, the food and service are generally first-rate.

AMERICAN

Budget meals

There are many places where you can get a soup, a sandwich, and salad for a tight-budget lunch in the downtown business area bounded by Pennsylvania Avenue, M Street, 14th Street, and 21st Street. They serve mostly office workers and are usually open only on weekdays for breakfast and lunch. Au Bon Pain has many locations around town, including 1801 L Street NW, 1401 I Street NW, 1850 M Street NW, and 706 L'Enfant Plaza SW.

AMERICA ($$)
Right in the middle of the hubbub of Union Station, America is an oasis with a something-for-everyone multiregion menu. Southwest specialties are its strong suit.
J4 Union Station, 50 Massachusetts Avenue NE
202/682–9555 Daily lunch and dinner Union Station

CLYDE'S ($–$$)
A long-time fixture in Georgetown (and other locations in the area), this is where to find your basic steak, burgers, and fish.
D3 3236 M Street NW
202/333–9180 Daily lunch and dinner; Sat, Sun breakfast
No nearby Metro

GEORGIA BROWN'S ($$)
This elegant New Southern restaurant, with its conversation nooks, is beloved by government officials, lobbyists, and journalists. Pork, lima beans, and okra are delicious here.
G4 950 15th Street NW
202/393–4499 Closed Sat, Sun McPherson Square

HARD ROCK CAFÉ ($)
This international chain celebrates the world of rock music. The rather ordinary menu scores for hamburgers and cherry pie.
G4 999 E Street NW
202/737–ROCK Daily lunch and dinner Metro Center

THE MONOCLE ($$$)
With fireplaces and many photos of politicians adorning the walls, this is one of the best restaurants for spotting members of Congress at lunch and dinner. The food is American with a Continental touch.
J5 107 D Street NE
202/546–4488 Closed Sat lunch and Sun Union Station

OLD EBBITT GRILL ($$)
One block from the White House, this is one of Washington's busiest restaurants, with oyster bar, pub food, and family fare.
G4 675 15th Street NW
202/347–4800 Daily breakfast, lunch, and dinner
Metro Center

OLD GLORY ($$)
The flags of six big barbecue-eating Southern states hang from the ceiling in this popular (and usually crowded) updated roadhouse, which serves all variations of barbecued pork, beef, and chicken.
D3 3139 M Street NW
202/337–3406 Daily lunch and dinner

PLANET HOLLYWOOD ($)
Owned by movie stars Bruce Willis, Demi Moore, Sylvester Stallone, and Arnold Schwarzenegger, this famous chain is to movies what the Hard Rock Café is to music. The menu includes beef, turkey, and vegetarian burgers and desserts such as Arnie's mother's apple strudel.
G5 1101 Pennsylvania Avenue NW 202/783–STAR
Daily lunch and dinner
Federal Triangle

INDIAN, AFRICAN, & MIDDLE EASTERN

ADITI ($)
This elegant, two-level Indian restaurant, with burgundy carpets and chairs, and pale mint-colored walls with brass sconces, serves high-quality breads and curries. The second floor overlooks Georgetown's busy M Street.
D3 3299 M Street NW 202/625–6825 Daily lunch and dinner

BACCHUS ($$)
An intimate Lebanese restaurant in an English basement; you can easily put together a meal from the long list of appetizers.
F3 1827 Jefferson Place NW 202/785–0734 Closed Sat lunch and Sun Dupont Circle

THE BOMBAY CLUB ($$)
Located just a block from the White House, this beautiful Indian restaurant, with its potted palms and a bright blue ceiling over white plaster moldings, tries to recapture the feel of a private club for British colonials in 19th-century India. The breads are first-rate, and seafood dishes, such as lobster Malabar, help justify the expense.
F4 815 Connecticut Avenue NW 202/659–3727 Daily dinner; Mon–Fri lunch; Sun brunch Farragut West

BUKOM CAFÉ ($)
Sunny African pop music, a palm-frond-and-kente-cloth decor, and a spicy West African menu with goat, lamb, chicken, and vegetable entrées brighten this narrow two-story dining room. There is live music nightly, and they serve food until late.
F2 2442 18th Street NW 202/265–4600 Tue–Sun dinner. Closed Mon Woodley Park–Zoo (6 blocks)

MARRAKESH ($$)
Located on a block of auto repair and supply shops, this Moroccan restaurant features a fixed-price feast shared by everyone at your table and eaten without cutlery. Belly dancers put on a nightly show.
H4 617 New York Avenue NW 202/393–9393 Closed lunch Gallery Place–Chinatown

SKEWERS ($)
As the name suggests, the specialty of this Middle Eastern restaurant is kabobs—meat, vegetable, or shrimp—served with almond-flaked rice or pasta. If Skewer's is too crowded, try the California eats downstairs at Café Luna (202/387–4005) or the reading room/coffee house upstairs at Luna Books (202/332–2543).
F3 1633 P Street NW 202/387–7400 Daily lunch and dinner Dupont Circle

ZED'S ETHIOPIAN CUISINE ($)
One of many Ethiopian restaurants in the city, this Georgetown outpost stakes its claim not with its simple decor but with its tangy *njera*, a bubbly bread used to dip into spicy meat and vegetable stews.
D3 3318 M Street NW 202/333–4710 Daily lunch and dinner.

Adams-Morgan eating

Adams-Morgan, the most ethnically diverse part of town, is a crowded, bustling, and interesting neighborhood, filled with a variety of restaurants. A walk along 18th Street will take you past Saigonnais (Vietnamese, 2307 18th Street), Argentine Grill (Argentine, 2433 18th Street), Meskerem (Ethiopian, 2434 18th Street), Montego Café (Jamaican, 2437 18th Street), the Star of Siam (Vietnamese, 2446 18th Street), Fasika's (Ethiopian, 2447 18th Street) and Straits of Malaya (Indonesian, 1836 18th Street).

ORIENTAL

Chinatown

Washington's Chinatown is a several-block area around 7th and H Streets NW. The area is somewhat run down, but there are some good restaurants, including Hunan Chinatown (✉ 624 H Street NW), Mr Yung's (✉ 740 6th Street NW), China Inn (✉ 631 H Street NW), Tony Cheng's Mongolian Restaurant (✉ 619 H Street NW) and Full Kee (✉ 509 H Street NW). A few other ethnic restaurants have entered the area, including Burma (✉ 740 6th Street NW upstairs), serving Burmese food, of course.

BENKAY ($$)
You can order from the menu, but the main attraction here is the buffet of sushi, tempura, and other Japanese foods, available at lunch and dinner.
G4 ✉ 727 15th Street NW, lower level ☎ 202/737–1515 Closed weekend lunch McPherson Square

BUSARA ($$)
A Thai restaurant, stylish in black rubber, brushed steel, and lacquer tables, that stands out of the crowd with unusual items, such as red curry duck and cellophone noodles with three kinds of mushroom.
C2 ✉ 2340 Wisconsin Avenue NW ☎ 202/337–2340 Daily lunch and dinner

CAFE ASIA ($)
The decor is spartan and the staff few, but low prices and the choice of cuisines —Singaporean, Indonesian, Japanese, Thai, Chinese, and Vietnamese—make the wait worthwhile.
F3 ✉ 1134 19th Street NW ☎ 202/659–2696 Closed Sun lunch Dupont Circle

LITTLE VIET GARDEN ($)
This and the nearby Queen Bee (3181 Wilson Boulevard, ☎ 703/527–3444) are among the many Vietnamese restaurants to be found in Arlington, VA. The Little Viet Garden has terrace dining in season.
A5 ✉ 3012 Wilson Boulevard, Arlington, VA ☎ 703/522–9686 Daily lunch and dinner

OODLES NOODLES ($)
Japanese udon, ramen, and egg and rice noodles in soups and as entrées in Malaysian, Indonesian, Japanese, Thai and Chinese cuisine.
F4 ✉ 1120 19th Street NW ☎ 202/293–3138 Closed Sun Farragut North

SAIGON GOURMET ($$)
Service is brisk and friendly at this popular, French-influenced, Vietnamese dining room; try the grilled pork with rice crêpes.
E1 ✉ 2635 Connecticut Avenue NW ☎ 202/265–1360 Daily lunch and dinner Woodley Park–Zoo

SALA THAI ($$)
Mirrored walls and soft lights soften the ambience of this small downstairs Thai restaurant, where noodles and curries are favorites.
F3 ✉ 2016 P Street NW ☎ 202/872–1144 Daily lunch and dinner Dupont Circle

SARINAH SATAY HOUSE ($)
This delightful Indonesian restaurant resembles an indoor garden, with real trees growing through the ceiling. Satays, combination plates, and crisp *loempia*, are all featured on the menu.
D3 ✉ 1338 Wisconsin Avenue NW ☎ 202/337–2955 Closed Sun lunch and Mon

STAR OF SIAM ($$)
This Thai restaurant's dishes, including squid salad, are among the most reliable in the city.
F3 ✉ 1136 19th Street NW ☎ 202/785–2839 Closed Sun lunch Dupont Circle

Tex-Mex, Spanish, & Latin

AUSTIN GRILL ($)
Hot adobe pastels and Texas music set the scene at this popular spot, which draws a young crowd for sizzling *fajitas* (chicken or steak) and chips with salsa.
C2 · 2404 Wisconsin Avenue NW · 202/337–8080 · Daily lunch and dinner

COCO LOCO ($$$)
This is two restaurants in one: a tapas bar and a Brazilian *churrasqueria*—grilled meat brought to your table and sliced on your plate. Thu–Sat nights, half the restaurant is an upscale night club.
H4 · 810 7th Street NW · 202/289–2626 · Closed weekend lunch · Gallery Place–Chinatown

THE GRILL FROM IPANEMA ($$)
The menu at this Adams-Morgan restaurant focuses on Brazilian cuisine, from spicy seafood stews to hearty meat dishes. Try traditional *feijoada*, a stew of black beans, pork, and smoked meat, served Wed and Sat.
F2 · 1858 Columbia Road NW · 202/986–0757 · Closed Mon–Fri lunch · Woodley Park–Zoo (nine blocks)

JALEO ($$)
Entrées are available, but it is the hot and cold tapas that are the house specialty.
H5 · 480 7th Street NW · 202/628–7949 · Daily lunch and dinner · Archives–Navy Memorial

LAURIOL PLAZA ($$)
The specialties of this simply decorated Spanish/South American restaurant include gazpacho, *ceviche*, and tongue.
F2 · 1801 18th Street NW · 202/387–0035 · Daily lunch and dinner · Dupont Circle

PEYOTE CAFÉ ($)
Located below Roxanne Restaurant (from whose Southwestern menu you may order), this pub has standard Tex-Mex items as well as vegetarian dishes.
F2 · 2319 18th Street NW · 202/462–8330 · Closed weekday lunch · Woodley Park–Zoo (7 blocks)

RED SAGE ($$$)
A faux-adobe warren of dining rooms with unrestrained Southwestern decor. Peppers are in everything but desserts, and portions and prices are big. There is a chilli bar and café upstairs.
G4 · 605 14th Street NW · 202/638–4444 · Main dining room closed weekend lunch · Metro Center

TABERNA DEL ALABARDERO ($$$)
The formal dining room, high-class service, and plush Old World decor create a romantic setting for classic Spanish tapas and seafood paella.
F4 · 1776 I Street NW (entrance on 18th Street) · 202/429–2200 · Closed Sat lunch and Sun · Farragut West

Bethesda feasting

Bethesda, just across the District line in Maryland, has in the past few years become a veritable city of restaurants. There are at least two dining guides available, each listing about 175 establishments and including information on hours, attire, and parking. The *Bethesda Dining Guide* is free and is available from the Bethesda Urban Partnership (7908 Woodmont Avenue, Bethesda · 301/215 6660). Another, moderately priced, guide, *The World's Most Complete Guide to Bethesda's Restaurants*, is available at local bookstores and some CVS Pharmacies.

Shopping Districts, Malls, & Department Stores

ADAMS-MORGAN
Within three blocks of 18th Street NW and Columbia Road, the Bohemian, eccentric, multicultural Adams-Morgan district offers a bewildering range of experiences for the dedicated shopper. Antiques shops specializing in the 1950s, Afro-centric apparel and accessories, a Haitian art gallery, a kosher grocery, jewelry hand-crafted by local artisans, and Skynear and Company (☒ 1800 Wyoming Avenue NW ☎ 202/797–7160), the most unusual home decorating shop in the city, are all to be found here.

CITY PLACE MALL
Discounted brand-name merchandise can be found at Nordstrom Rack, Ross, Marshall's, Shoe Rack, Nine West, and four dozen other retailers; there are also 10 movie screens and a food court.
✚ Off map to north ☒ 8661 Colesville Road, Silver Spring MD ☎ 301/589–1091 🕐 Mon–Sat 10–9; Sun 12–6 🚇 Silver Spring

CONNECTICUT AVENUE
Connecticut Avenue above Dupont Circle provides a lively mix of restaurants and stores offering modern furniture, housewares, shoes, and gourmet coffee shops that support the bookstores lining the avenue. Connecticut below the circle is home to upscale department stores and boutiques, especially for women.

EASTERN MARKET
Gentrified Capitol Hill retains the Eastern Market, home on Saturday to a lively produce market and on Sunday to an open-air antiques and import bazaar. Surrounding the market are antique stores and secondhand clothing shops, one specializing in men's apparel. Here, too, the croissant and coffee culture has invaded, so you can get fresh roasted beans, brioche, and grilled vegetable sandwiches. For breakfast or lunch, don't overlook the Market Lunch, which provides old-style ham and eggs, enormous flapjacks with rich blueberry topping, and the city's best crab cakes.
✚ K6 ☒ Pennsylvania Avenue & 7th Street SE 🚇 Eastern Market

FASHION CENTER
Macy's and Nordstrom anchor the 160 shops at Fashion Center at Pentagon City. Nordstrom's practices are credited with reviving retail service in recent years. The clerks here know the stock intimately and are superbly trained to assist you, whether you are browsing, replacing a ripped stocking, or buying a fur coat. If you have hard-to-fit feet, try Nordstrom's, which

originally began life as a shoestore.
D8 ✉ 1100 S. Hayes Street at Army-Navy Drive and I-395 S ☎ 703/415-2400 Mon–Sat 10–9:30; Sun 11–6 Pentagon City

GEORGETOWN PARK
The spacious, posh, three-level Georgetown Park is a delight for anyone heading through the lively streets to Wisconsin and M, the heart of Georgetown shopping. Many galleries, antiques stores, and boutiques are within easy walking distance. The crowd jostling you on this corner is young, hip, and on its way up. There is a wide range of apparel and decorator shops for the tasteful and well-to-do.
D3 ✉ 3222 M Street NW ☎ 202/298-5577 Mon–Sat 10–9; Sun noon–6

HECHT AND COMPANY
Affectionately known as "Hecht's," this well-laid-out department store will satisfy diverse tastes, from conservative to trendy. There is also a walk-in Ticketmaster sales counter for area shows, concerts, and sports events at rock-bottom prices.
G4 ✉ 12th & G Streets NW ☎ 202/628-6661 Mon–Sat 9–8; Sun noon–6 Metro Center

MAZZA GALLERIE
Mazza Gallerie has the ritzy Neiman Marcus department store and a discount Filene's Basement, along with 40 other shops offering gourmet cookware (Williams-Sonoma, Laura Ashley Home), upscale women's shoes (Stephane Kélian), maternity wear for the very fashion conscious (Pea in the Pod), and one-of-a-kind furnishings and gifts with something of a Southwestern flavor (Skynear and Company).
Off map to north ✉ 5300 Wisconsin Avenue NW ☎ 202/686-9515 Mon–Fri 10–8; Sat 10–6; Sun noon–5 Friendship Heights

POTOMAC MILLS MALL
This is the local daddy of discount shopping and has now become the largest tourist attraction in Virginia. Specialty outlets such as Fossils and The Nature Company complement department stores Ikea, J.C. Penney, and Marshall's, 15 movie theaters, and a food court offering everything from ice cream to sushi. Potomac Mills is 30 miles south of D.C. off I-95
Off map to south ✉ 3900 Potomac Mills Circle, Prince William, VA ☎ 703/643-1770 Mon–Sat 10–9:30; Sun 11–6 Shuttle from D.C. ☎ 703/878-1262

Stay cool
Washington summers are only bearable because of air conditioning, and the malls crank up the coolers to accommodate shoppers, diners, and movie-goers. And there is always a sale. In the words of the "shop till you drop" crowd, "If you paid full price, you're not playing the game right."

BOOKS & MUSIC

Books for nightowls

You can find bookstores open well into the night in nearly every area of Washington, many with cafés, knowledgeable staff, and discounts. There is always a place to browse after a day's sightseeing or business meetings.

BOOKWORKS: WASHINGTON PROJECT FOR THE ARTS

Bookworks specializes in artists' books and books from small presses.
G5 400 7th Street NW 202/347–4590 Tue–Sat 11–6 Archives–Navy Memorial

BORDERS BOOKS AND MUSIC

Borders is a national chain, offering 325,000 titles (including 50,000 music titles), and leading the booksellers' industry by combining book and music sales, a café, daily readings, book signings, and literary and musical events. Helpful, knowledgeable staff encourage browsing, listening, and reading, in this spacious store.
F3 18th and L Streets, NW 202/466–4999 Mon–Fri 8AM–10PM; Sat 9–9; Sun 11–7 Farragut West

CHAPTERS LITERARY BOOKSTORE

Specializing in poetry, fiction, and literary criticism, Chapters takes books seriously: no cartoon books, just real books for readers.
F3 1512 K Street NW 202/347–5495 Mon–Fri 10–6:30; Sat 11–5 McPherson Square

CROWN BOOKS

This national chain specializes in bestsellers, crafts, popular psychology, fiction, and the "kiss'n'tell" books so loved by Washington scandal-mongers. Everything is heavily discounted, especially the overloaded remainders table at the front of every store.
F3 11 Dupont Circle NW 202/319–1374 Daily 9AM–midnight Dupont Circle; F4 2020 K Street NW 202/659–2030 Mon–Fri 9–7, Sat 10–6

KEMP MILL MUSIC

This local chain keeps prices low on a full range of CDs and tapes. Both branches are open Mon–Thu 10–10; Fri–Sat 10–midnight; Sun 11–7.
F2 2459 18th Street NW 202/387–1011 Dupont Circle. F4 1900 L Street NW 202/223–5310 Farragut West

KRAMERBOOKS & AFTERWORDS CAFÉ

This is the quintessential Washington literary pick-up scene and one of the oldest and most venerable booksellers.
F4 1517 Connecticut Avenue NW 202/387–1400 Weekends 24 hours; Mon–Thu 7:30AM–1AM Dupont Circle

LAMBDA RISING BOOK STORE

An intriguingly named store that offers gay and lesbian books and gifts.
E3 1625 Connecticut Avenue NW 202/462–6969 Daily 10–12 Dupont Circle

LAMMAS BOOKSTORE

A great selection of books by and for women.
E3 1426 21st Street NW 202/775–8218 Daily 11–8 Dupont Circle

MELODY RECORD SHOP

Knowledgeable staff and a 10 percent–40 percent

discount on CDs, cassettes, and tapes are particular attractions here.
F3 1623 Connecticut Avenue NW 202/232–4002 Mon–Thu 10–10; Fri–Sat 10AM–11PM; Sun 11–10 Farragut North

OLSSON'S BOOKS & RECORDS
A comprehensive stock covering most areas of publishing, plus folk and classical recordings in many formats.
D3 1239 Wisconsin Avenue, NW 202/338–9544 Mon–Thu 10AM–11PM; Fri–Sat 10AM–midnight; Sun 11–10

ORPHEUS RECORDS
This store stocks all styles of music in every format, but vinyl hunters will be attracted by high-quality used LPs and the best selection of new vinyl in the city especially rock and roll, jazz, and blues.
D3 3249 M Street NW 202/337–7970 Mon–Sat 11–11; Sun noon–8

POLITICS AND PROSE
This is the largest independent bookstore in the area. It offers comfortable reading chairs, a coffee shop, and knowledgeable staff.
Off map at E1 5015 Connecticut Avenue NW 202/364–1919 Sun–Thu 9AM–10:30PM; Fri–Sat 9–9 VanNess, then 15 minutes' walk north

SECOND STORY BOOKS
If used books are your passion, start here. If you don't find your treasure on the acres of shelves, it may be in Second Story's warehouse. They also offer a very helpful nationwide search service for out-of-print books.
F3 2000 P Street NW 202/659–8884 Daily 10–10 Dupont Circle

SERENADE RECORD SHOP
A store that is strong on classical but carries almost everything else in all formats, except LPs.
F3 1800 M Street NW 202/452–0075 Mon–Sat 9–6

SISTER'S SPACE & BOOKS
A specialist store for books by and about African-American women.
G2 1354 U Street NW 202/332–3433 Tue–Sat 10–7; Sun noon–5 U Street–Cardozo

TOWER RECORDS
Loud and hip, here is the largest selection of cassettes and CDs in Washington. The selection covers jazz, rock, soul, and classical.
E4 2000 Pennsylvania Avenue NW 202/331–2400 Daily 9AM–midnight Foggy Bottom

U.S. GOVERNMENT BOOKSTORE
Here are the countless publications produced by the Feds, including research reports on American history, home improvements, internal revenue studies, energy, environmental improvements, health, and nutrition.
G4 1510 H Street NW 202/653–5075 Mon–Fri 8:30–4:30 McPherson Square

Special-interest tomes

Specialty books can be located in the hundreds of professional associations, think tanks, and foundations that make Washington home—the Brookings Institution, the Carnegie Endowment for International Peace, the Freedom Forum, the American Association of Museums, the American Institute of Architects, and even the American Society of Association Executives. If you've got an interest in architecture, bee-keeping, chemistry, or zoology, you can find both popular and scholarly editions to inform and challenge every aspect of your passion.

Vintage Secondhand Shopping & Museum Shops

Tax-exempt shopping

Even tiny museums and historic houses carefully create retail space. Cedar Hill, for instance, offers a wide selection of books on African-American history. Because these are nonprofit tax-exempt organizations, the customer is not charged sales tax at museum shops, making a saving of 7 percent on all purchases.

MUSEUM SHOPS

The gift shops of Washington's museums offer some of the best shopping anywhere, and no serious shopper should overlook them. The Smithsonian is the area's third-largest retailer.

In addition to bookstores geared to a museum's topic —modern art, African culture, American politics and history, architecture, or whatever—museum shops offer reproduction furnishings and decorative arts, jewelry, and apparel related to the museum's collection. The Hirshhorn Museum offers modern jewelry; the National Museum of American History has reproduction 19th-century toys, kitchen-ware, and hand-made quilts; the Corcoran Museum offers blown-glass objects and woven scarves; the Building Museum sells tools and architectural puzzles.

Alphabets and cartoon animation can be bought from a tiny area at the front desk of the National Children's Museum. The Department of Interior acts as an outlet for Native American art and crafts. Bonsai pots and pruning gear can be found at the National Arboretum and herbs from the Bishop's Garden at Washington National Cathedral. Hillwood offers Russian icons, porcelain, cloisonné, and Native American dream-catchers and pottery. The latest stamps can be purchased and posted at the National Postal Museum. Kids love the dried ice creams at the National Air and Space Museum and the dinosaurs at the National Museum of Natural History. Souvenir T-shirts can be found everywhere to fit every taste and body form.

ONCE IS NOT ENOUGH

Come here for used but stylish men's, women's and children's clothing and accessories at terrific prices.

A2 · 4830 MacArthur Boulevard NW · 202/337–3072 · Mon–Sat 10–5

THE OPPORTUNITY SHOP OF THE CHRIST CHILD SOCIETY

Operated for charitable purposes, this store sells vintage clothing, good-quality housewares, and consigned antiques.

D3 · 1427 Wisconsin Avenue NW · 202/333–6635 · Tue–Sat 10–3:45

SECONDI

This second-floor consignment shop in the heart of Dupont Circle features fashions from the Gap to Chanel for both men and women.

F3 · 1702 Connecticut Avenue NW · 202/667–1122 · Mon–Sat 11–6; Sun 1–5 · Dupont Circle

UNIFORM

Uniform traps you in time: feathered mules with lucite heels, knee-high full skirts, three-button suits, clutch bags, lava lamps, and chunky plastic jewelry.

F2 · 2407 18th Street NW · 202/483–4577 · Mon–Sat 11–8; Sun noon–7 · Dupont Circle

Antiques, Crafts, & Collectibles

THE AMERICAN HAND
This gallery-shop sells one-of-a-kind and limited-edition ceramics, textiles, and wood crafts.
E3 2906 M Street NW 202/965–3273 Mon–Sat 11–6; Sun 1–5

APPALACHIAN SPRING
Seek this out for ceramics, quilts, fine woodwork, and other traditional and contemporary crafts.
D3 1415 Wisconsin Avenue NW 202/337–5780 Mon–Sat 10–6; Sun 12–5

CHENONCEAU ANTIQUES
Here are American 19th- and 20th-century antiques chosen by someone with a sophisticated knowledge of this period.
F2 2314 18th Street NW 202/667–1651 Thu–Sun

CHERISHABLES
Cherishables emphasizes 18th-century Federal furniture and decorations.
F3 1608 20th Street NW 202/785 4087 Mon–Sat 11–6

GEORGETOWN ANTIQUES CENTER
Victorian art nouveau and art deco objects are displayed in an accommodating Victorian townhouse.
E3 2918 M Street NW 202/338–3811 Mon–Sat 11–6; Sun noon–5

G.K.S. BUSH
Browse among early American high-style furniture and related art.
E3 2828 Pennsylvania Avenue NW 202/965–0653 Mon–Fri 10–6; Sat 10–5

INDIAN CRAFT SHOP
This shop showcases hand-crafted Eskimo walrus-ivory carving, Zuni pots, Hopi dolls, and Navajo pottery.
F5 Department of Interior, 1849 C Street NW, Room 1023 202/208–4056 Mon–Fri 8:30–4:30 McPherson Square

MARSTON LUCE
This gallery is chock full of American folk art, weathervanes, and geometric textiles.
F5 1314 21st Street NW 202/775–9460 Mon–Sat 11–6

THE PHOENIX
The place to come for Mexican folk crafts, silver jewelry, and natural-fiber native and contemporary clothing.
D3 1514 Wisconsin Avenue NW 202/338–4404 Mon–Sat 10–6; Sun 11–5

RETROSPECTIVE
Retrospective sells the things baby-boomers grew up on in the 1940s and 1950s: streamlined designs in metal furniture, clunky tableware, and bold patterns.
F2 2324 18th Street NW 202/483–8112 Mon–Fri noon–7; Sat 11–7; Sun noon–6. Closed Tue

SUSQUEHANNA
Susquehanna specializes in American furniture and works of art in the largest antique space in Georgetown.
D3 3216 O Street NW 202/333–1511 Mon–Sat 10–6

Treasure-hunting

Georgetown, Adams-Morgan, Dupont Circle, and the 7th Street art corridor are abundantly supplied with galleries, boutiques, and specialty stores. An afternoon shopping excursion will no doubt yield trinkets and treasures for the entire family.

Clothing

Understated elegance

Washingtonians cultivate a studied dowdiness of dress. High-fashion shopping is limited to the Watergate and Willard hotels, but if you want office or tourist attire, you can get great buys almost everywhere.

BRITCHES OF GEORGETOWN

Stylish men come to the two branches of this store for trendy but traditional clothing in natural fibers.
F3 1219 Connecticut Avenue NW 202/347–8994 Mon–Wed, Fri, Sat 10–6; Thu 10–8 Dupont Circle D3 1247 Wisconsin Avenue NW 202/338–3330 Mon–Wed, Fri, Sat 10–7; Thu 10–9; Sun 12–6 No nearby Metro

BROOKS BROTHERS

A real institution, Brooks is the oldest men's specialty store in the nation: it began outfitting American men in 1818.
F4 1840 L Street NW 202/659–4650 Mon–Wed, Fri, Sat 9:30–6; Thu 9:30–7; Sun 12–5 Farragut West

BURBERRYS

The store that introduced Americans to the trenchcoat; the British company also manufactures traditional, high-quality apparel.
F3 1155 Connecticut Avenue NW 202/463–3000 Mon–Wed, Fri, Sat 9:30–6; Thu 9:30–7; Sun noon–5 Dupont Circle

CHANEL

Chanel has its largest store in America, full of pricey, desirable women's clothes and accessories, at the Willard Hotel.
G4 1455 Pennsylvania Avenue, NW 202/638–5055 Mon–Sat 10–6 Metro Center

FORECAST

Forecast's experienced buyer works hard for the individualistic females who frequent this shop.
K6 218 7th Street SE 202/547–7337 Tue–Fri 11–7; Sat 10–6; Sun 12–5 Eastern Market

J. PRESS

J. Press has provided the Ivy League look since 1902, when it was founded at Yale University.
F4 1801 L Street NW 202/857–0120 Mon–Sat 9:30–6 Farragut West

KHISMET WEARABLE ART

Original designs and African fabrics create unusual and beautiful day and evening wear for women.
F2 1800 Belmont Road NW 202/234–7778 Wed–Sat 1–8; Sun 1–6 Dupont Circle

KOBOS

Kobos imports West African clothing, accessories, and African music.
F2 2444 18th Street NW 202/332–9580 Mon–Sat 11–7; Sun 12–6 Dupont Circle

RIZIK BROTHERS

Designer clothing combines with expert service in this famous Washington ladies' outfitters.
F3 1100 Connecticut Avenue NW 202/223–4050 Mon–Sat 9–6; Thu until 8 Farragut North

TOAST & STRAWBERRIES

Original clothing from around the world is sold with art work and art wear.
F3 1608 20th Street NW 202/234–1212 Mon–Sat 11–7; Sun 1–6 Dupont Circle

Gourmet Foods & Specialty Stores

DEAN & DELUCA

Occupying one of the 19th-century farmers' markets on Georgetown's main street, this New York export store offers thousands of high-quality products, from bakery goods and double-fat cheese to designer vegetables, salads, and elegant entrées for one or many.
D3 3276 M Street NW 202/342–2500 Sun–Thu 10–8; Fri, Sat 10–9

EASTERN MARKET

Eastern Market, unrestored and retaining its neighborhood character, sells the freshest produce to be had in the city, particularly during harvest seasons, when farmers from Maryland and Virginia come to market on Saturday morning. On Sunday the tin-roofed arcade shelters a lively flea market.
K6 7th and C Streets SE 202/546–2698 Tue–Sat 7–6; Sun 9–4 Eastern Market

THE FRENCH MARKET

This market has been educating the local palate for 50 years. Home-made pâtés, escargots, baguettes, croissants, and French cheeses.
D2 1626-32 Wisconsin Avenue NW 202/338–4828 Tue–Sat 8:30–6

FRESH FIELDS WHOLE FOODS MARKET

This small national chain succeeded in a saturated market because of absolute top-quality, mostly organic, fresh foods with old-fashioned customer service. The oatmeal cookies with maple sugar icing can't be beat, at any price!
Off map C1 to northwest 4530 40th Street NW 202/237–5800 Mon–Sat 8AM–10PM; Sun 8–8 Tenley Town

A LITTERI

At this location since 1932, this Italian specialty shop is in the heart of the capital city's wholesale food market, worth the short cab ride necessary from downtown D.C. Litteri's features more than 40 brands of imported olive oil and wines to go with every pasta dish known to mankind.
K3 517 Morse Street NE 202/544–0183 Tue–Wed 8–4; Thur–Fri 8–5; Sat 8–3

LAWSON'S

Lawson's caters to a single professional population with home-made salads, prepared entrées, salad bar, wine selections, and full bakery.
F3 1350 Connecticut Avenue NW 202/775–0400 Mon–Fri 7:30–8; Sat 10–6 Dupont Circle

RED SAGE GENERAL STORE

An outgrowth of the popular Southwestern restaurant next door, this store sells chillies and hot-hot-hot to mild salsa, fancy olive oils and herbal vinegars, fresh-baked breads, and desserts.
G4 14th and F streets NW 202/638–3276 Mon–Sun 8–5:30 Metro Center

The specialty boom

Specialty food stores have arrived, in essence replacing local produce markets that once supplied the populace. A recent phenomenon is the coffee bar, a Seattle export that seems to have invaded the city in the past few years. You can get your tall double de-caf with a twist on almost any corner.

THEATERS

Tickets

Tickets to most events are available at the box office or through one of three main ticket outlets. TicketMaster (202/432–7328) sells tickets by phone or at selected stores to concerts, sports events, and many special events. Protix (703/218–6500) has tickets to shows at Wolf Trap and some other venues. TicketPlace (202/842–5387) sells half-price, day-of-performance tickets for selected shows (it is also a full-price TicketMaster outlet). Tickets must be bought in person at Lisner Auditorium 730 21st Street NW Tue–Fri noon–6; Sat 11–5; tickets for Sun and Mon performances sold on Sat. Only cash is accepted; there is a 10 percent service charge per order.

ARENA STAGE

Arena manages a long season in its three theaters: the theatre-in-the-round Arena, the proscenium Kreeger, and the cabaret-style Old Vat Room. The New Voices series offers reduced prices to see developing shows.
H7 6th Street and Maine Avenue SW 202/488–3300 Waterfront

FORD'S THEATER

Now mostly presenting musicals (Dickens's *A Christmas Carol* is presented at Christmas every year), this is the theater where President Abraham Lincoln was assassinated.
G4 511 10th Street NW 202/347–4833 Metro Center

GALA HISPANIC THEATER

This company presents Spanish classics, as well as contemporary and modern Latin-American plays in both Spanish and English.
F1 1625 Park Road NW 202/234–7174

KENNEDY CENTER

Kennedy Center is Washington's busiest cultural center, hosting a wide variety of events, including ballet, modern dance, drama, and experimental theater.
E4 New Hampshire Avenue and Rock Creek Parkway 202/467–4600 or 800/444–1324 Foggy Bottom

NATIONAL THEATER

Destroyed by fire and rebuilt four times, the National Theater has operated in the same location since 1835. It presents pre- and post-Broadway shows.
G4 1321 Pennsylvania Avenue NW 202/628–6161 Metro Center

SHAKESPEARE THEATER

The Shakespeare's season includes four plays, three by the Bard and one by one of his contemporaries.
H5 450 7th Street NW 202/393–2700 Archives–Navy Memorial

SOURCE THEATER

The 107-seat Source Theater presents established plays and modern interpretations of classics. Each July and August, Source hosts a series of new plays, many by local playwrights.
G2 1835 14th Street NW 202/462–1073 U Street– Cardozo

STUDIO THEATER

One of Washington's nicest independent company theaters, Studio performs a mix of classics and offbeat plays. The 50-seat Secondstage presents experimental works.
G3 1333 P Street NW 202/332–3300 Dupont Circle

WARNER THEATER

After a two-year major restoration, the Warner reopened in 1992 and now hosts theater and dance performances, as well as some pop music shows.
G4 13th and E Streets NW 202/783–4000 Metro Center

Concert Halls

DAR CONSTITUTION HALL
Formerly home to the National Symphony Orchestra, this 3,700-seat hall hosts musical performances, staged shows, and the occasional big-name comedy act.
F5 18th and D Streets NW 202/638–2661 Farragut West (6 blocks north)

GEORGE MASON UNIVERSITY
The GMU campus in suburban Virginia is home to the Center for the Arts. The Patriot Center, also on campus, holds concerts and sporting events.
Off map to south Route 123 and Braddock Road, Fairfax, VA Center for the Arts: 703/993–8888; Patriot Center: 703/993–3000 or 202/432–7328

LISNER AUDITORIUM
This 1,500-seat theater, located on the campus of George Washington University, presents pop, classical, and choral music performances.
F4 21st and H Streets NW 202/994–1500 Foggy Bottom

MERRIWEATHER POST PAVILION
Located one hour north of Washington, this outdoor pavilion with some covered seating hosts big-name pop acts during the summer months.
Off map to north Columbia, MD 301/982–1800 or 301/596–0660

NATIONAL GALLERY OF ART
The National Gallery Orchestra, as well as outside recitalists and ensembles, holds free concerts in the West Building's West Garden Court on Sunday evenings from October to June.
H5 6th Street and Constitution Avenue NW 202/842–6941 Archives–Navy Memorial

NISSAN PAVILION AT STONE RIDGE
This 25,000-seat venue opened in 1995 near Manassas, VA, about one hour from Washington.
Off map to south 7800 Cellar Door Drive, Gainesville, VA 703/549–7625 or 202/432–7328

SMITHSONIAN INSTITUTION
A wide assortment of music—both free and ticketed—is presented by the Smithsonian at various indoor and outdoor locations. The Smithsonian Associates Program (202/357–3030) offers everything from acappella groups to Cajun zydeco bands, as well as other kinds of event.
G5, H5, H4 At various Smithsonian museums, most of which are on the Mall 202/357–2700 Smithsonian

USAIR ARENA
This 18,000-seat arena is one of the area's top venues for big-name pop, rock, and rap acts.
Off map to east 1 Harry S Truman Drive, Landover, MD 301/350–3400 or 202/432–7328

Kennedy Center

The Kennedy Center (► 25) is indeed a center for cultural events, with five separate stages under one roof: the Concert Hall, home to the National Symphony Orchestra; the Opera House, the stage for ballet, modern dance, grand opera, and large-scale musicals; the Eisenhower Theater, usually used for drama; the Terrace Theater, a smaller stage for chamber groups and experimental works; and the Theater Lab.

BARS & LOUNGES

Where the action is

Washington has many pockets of activity, mostly centered within the downtown business district or more ethnically diverse neighborhoods. Adams-Morgan, around 18th Street and Columbia Road, has many bars, clubs, and restaurants. Capitol Hill (especially along Pennsylvania Avenue SE), the U Street NW corridor (from about 14th Street to 18th Street), and the downtown area around 19th and M Streets NW, are also fairly dense with similar night activities.

Listings

The Washington Post is the leading daily. The Friday "Weekend" section lists entertainment and special events. The Sunday edition carries a guide to the "lively arts." The *City Paper*, delivered on Thursdays, is a free alternative weekly with the best calendar of current events. The monthly *Washingtonian Magazine* reviews restaurants and performances and provides in-depth coverage of the city.

BRICKSKELLER
With almost 700 brands of beer for sale, from Central American lagers to U.S. microbrewed ales, this is Washington's premier pub. Bartenders oblige beer-can collectors by opening the containers from the bottom.
E3 1523 22nd Street NW 202/293–1885 Mon–Thu 11:30AM–2AM; Fri 11:30AM–3AM; Sat 6AM–3AM; Sun 6PM–2AM Dupont Circle

CAPITOL CITY BREWING COMPANY
This microbrewery, the first brewery in Washington since Prohibition, features a gleaming copper bar, with metal steps leading up to where the brews are actually made. Capitol City makes everything from a bitter to a bock, though not all types are available at all times.
G4 1100 New York Avenue NW 202/628– 2222 Mon–Sat 11AM–2AM; Sun 11AM–midnight Metro Center

CHAMPIONS
One of D.C.'s biggest sports bars, the walls are covered with jerseys, pucks, bats, and balls, and the evening's big game is always on the big screen.
D3 1206 Wisconsin Avenue NW 202/965–4005 Mon–Thu 5AM–2AM; Fri 5PM–3AM; Sat 11:30AM–3AM; Sun 11:30AM–2AM. One-drink minimum Fri and Sat after 10PM.

THE DUBLINER
The closest thing in Washington to an Irish pub, this is a favorite with Capitol Hill staffers.
J4 520 North Capitol Road NW 202/737–3773 Sun–Thu 11AM–1:30AM; Fri–Sat 11.M–2:30AM Union Station

HAWK'N'DOVE
A friendly neighborhood bar, frequented mostly by political types, lobbyists, and marines (from a nearby barracks).
J6 329 Pennsylvania Avenue SE 202/543–3300 Sun–Thu 10AM–2AM; Fri–Sat 10AM–3AM Capitol South

OZIO
One of the most popular spots for the latest trend in clubs, the cigar-and-martini bar.
F4 1835 K Street NW 202/822–6000 Sun–Thu noon–2AM; Fri–Sat noon–3AM Farragut North or Farragut West

SIGN OF THE WHALE
This well-known post-Preppie/neo-Yuppie haven is right in the heart of a densely bar-populated area of downtown.
F3 1825 M Street NW 202/785–1110 Sun–Thu 11:30AM–2AM; Fri–Sat 11:30AM–3AM Farragut North

YACHT CLUB
Just across the border into Maryland, this lounge is popular with well-dressed, middle-aged singles. Jacket and tie or turtleneck required (casual Wed).
Off map to northwest 8111 Woodmont Avenue, Bethesda, MD 301/654–2396 Tue–Thu 5PM–1AM; Fri 5PM–2AM; Sat 8AM–2AM.

NIGHTCLUBS (LIVE MUSIC)

THE BAYOU
This longtime Georgetown rock club showcases national acts and local talent. Every variety of rock music is covered. Tickets are available at the door or through TicketMaster. Occasional no-alcohol, all-ages shows give those under 18 a chance to dance. Cover charge. No credit cards.
D4 3135 K Street NW 202/333–2897 Generally open daily 8PM–2AM

BIRCHMERE
The best place in the area to hear nationally known acoustic folk and bluegrass acts, with the occasional rockabilly or rock act.
Off map 3701 Mount Vernon Avenue, Alexandria, VA 703/549–7500 Sun–Thu 6:30PM–11PM; Fri–Sat 7PM–12:30AM

BLUES ALLEY
Washington's best jazz club, Blues Alley serves up national jazz acts, such as Ramsey Lewis and Charlie Byrd, as well as Creole cooking. Cover charge and minimum charge.
D3 Rear 1073 Wisconsin Avenue NW 202/337–4141 Sun–Thu 6PM–midnight; Fri and Sat 6PM–2AM. Shows at 8 and 10, plus occasional midnight shows Fri and Sat

CAFÉ LAUTREC
They play jazz every night in this club with Toulouse-Lautrec decor and French food. Come on Friday or Saturday and watch tap dancer Johne Forges dance on the tabletops. Minimum charge applies Tue and Thu–Sun.
F2 2431 18th Street NW 202/265–6436 Sun–Thu 5PM–2AM; Fri–Sat 5PM–3AM

9:30 CLUB
This trendy club is dark, hot in summer, cold in winter and always smoky, but it has possibly the best array of local, national, and international progressive music. Cover charge. Get tickets at the door or from TicketMaster.
G4 815 V Street NW 202/393–0930 Generally open Sun–Thu 7:30PM–midnight; Fri–Sat 9PM–2AM Metro Center

ONE STEP DOWN
Like a good jazz club should be, One Step Down is smoky, low-ceilinged, and intimate, with the best jazz jukebox in town. It books many local acts and often features New York jazz artists. Live music is presented Wed–Sat. Cover charge and minimum charge.
E4 2517 Pennsylvania Avenue NW 202/331–8863 Mon–Thu 10AM–2AM; Fri 10AM–3AM; Sat noon–3AM; Sun noon–2AM Foggy Bottom

TWIST AND SHOUT
This club is one of the best spots for "roots" music, such as Cajun, zydeco, blues, and rockabilly.
off map 4800 Auburn Avenue, Bethesda 301/652–3383 Variable hours: generally open Thu–Sun night

Night options

Washington clubs offer every kind of music. You can have it live or played by a DJ. There can be dancing or just listening. Or check out one of the murder mystery dinners, whodunits where the audience gets involved with the story while watching it. The Blair Mansion Inn (7711 Eastern Avenue, Silver Spring, MD 301/588–1689) and the Murder Mystery Dinner Theater (Old Europe, 2434 Wisconsin Avenue NW 202/333–6875) have weekend shows.

Miscellaneous Arts

Movies

Check the daily newspapers for mainstream first-run movies; cinemas are scattered throughout the city. For revivals and foreign, independent, and avant-garde films, try the American Film Institute ✉ Kennedy Center ☎ 202/785–4600 and the Key ✉ 1222 Wisconsin Avenue NW ☎ 202/333–5100. The Hirshhorn Museum ☎ 202/357–2700, National Gallery of Art East Building ☎ 202/737–4215, and National Archives ☎ 202/501–5000, all on the Mall, often show historical, unusual, or experimental films. Filmfest D.C. ☎ 202/274–6810, an annual citywide festival of international cinema, takes place in late April and early May.

American folklife

The Smithsonian's Festival of American Folklife provides an alternative to high culture and fine art. Each year the Smithsonian celebrates one country, one state, one profession, and a number of musical folk traditions. Summer temperatures persuade bureaucrats and others to join in the early evening, open-air dance parties enjoyed by all ages.

CHAMBER MUSIC

Corcoran Gallery of Art ✉ 17th Street and New York Avenue NW ☎ 202/639–1700 🕐 One Friday each month, Oct– May, plus some summer dates

Folger Shakespeare Library The Folger Consort plays medieval, Renaissance, and baroque music ✉ 201 East Capitol Street SE ☎ 202/544–7077 🕐 Oct–May

National Academy of Sciences Free performances Oct–May ✉ 2101 Constitution Avenue NW ☎ 202/334–2436 🕐 Oct–May Free

Phillips Collection ✉ 1600 21st Street NW ☎ 202/387–2151 🕐 Sep–May, Sun at 5PM

CHORAL GROUPS

Choral Arts Society A 180-voice choir performs at the Kennedy Center (➤ 25) ☎ 202/244–3669 🕐 Sep–Jun, plus three Xmas sing-alongs in Dec

Washington National Cathedral Choral and church groups frequently perform in the cathedral (➤ 59) ☎ 202/537–6200

National Shrine of the Immaculate Conception Venue for choral groups (➤ 47) ☎ 202/526–8300

COMEDY CLUBS

Capitol Steps Political musical revue most weekends at Chelsea's ✉ 1055 Thomas Jefferson Street NW ☎ 202/298–8222

Gross National Product Political satire Saturdays at the Bayou ✉ 3135 K Street NW ☎ 202/783–7212 or 202/333–2897 🕐 Sat

The Improv Well-known comedians ✉ 1140 Connecticut Avenue NW ☎ 202/296–7008

CONCERT SERIES

Armed Forces Concert Series East Terrace of the Capitol and the Sylvan Theater in the Washington Monument grounds ☎ 202/767–5658 (Air Force) ☎ 703/696–3399 (Army) ☎ 202/433–2525 (Navy) ☎ 202/433–4011 (Marines) 🕐 Jun–Aug weekday evenings

Carter Barron Amphitheater Pop, jazz, and gospel music. During two weeks in June the Shakespeare Theater (➤ 78) presents a free play by the Bard in this outdoor spot ✉ 16th Street and Colorado Avenue NW ☎ 202/426–6837 🕐 Mid-Jun–Aug, Sat and Sun evenings

Washington Performing Arts Society Books performers in halls around the city ☎ 202/833–9800

DANCE

Dance Place Modern and ethnic dance ✉ 3225 8th Street NE ☎ 202/269–1600 🕐 Most weekends

Joy of Motion The home of several area troupes ✉ 1643 Connecticut Avenue NW ☎ 202/387–0911

Mount Vernon College Hosts visiting dance companies in the autumn and spring ✉ 2100 Foxhall Road NW ☎ 202/625–4655

Smithsonian Associates Program Dance groups performing at various Smithsonian museums ☎ 202/357–3030

The Washington Ballet Various ballet performances, plus *The Nutcracker* in December ☎ 202/362–3606 🕐 Oct, Feb, May and Dec

Sports

BIKING

For information on bike trails in and around Washington, contact the Washington Area Bicyclist Association (✉ 818 Connecticut Avenue NW, Suite 300, 20006 ☎ 202/872–9830, fax 202/833–4626). Some of the best rides are along the George Washington Memorial Parkway, which runs along the Virginia side of the Potomac River all the way to Mount Vernon (35 miles round-trip); on the C & O Canal towpath from Georgetown to Cumberland, MD (180 miles one-way); and through Rock Creek Park).

Rent bikes from **Bicycle Exchange** (near the Mount Vernon Trail) ✉ 1506-C Belle View Boulevard, Alexandria, VA ☎ 703/768–3444 **Big Wheel Bikes** (near the C & O Canal towpath) ✉ 1034 33rd Street NW, Georgetown ☎ 202/337–0254 **City Bikes** (near the Rock Creek bike path) ✉ 2501 Champlain Street NW ☎ 202/265–1564 **Fletcher's Boat House** ✉ C & O Canal towpath, 2 miles north of Georgetown, near Reservoir Road NW ☎ 202/244–0461 **Metropolis Bicycles** (also rents Rollerblades) ✉ 709 8th Street SE, Capitol Hill ☎ 202/543–8900 **Thompson's Boat Center** ✉ Virginia Avenue and Rock Creek Park, behind Kennedy Center ☎ 202/333–4861

BOATING

Fletcher's Boat House (see Biking, left), rents rowboats and canoes. **Thompson's Boat Center** (at Virginia Avenue and Rock Creek Parkway behind the Kennedy Center) rents canoes, rowboats, rowing shells, and sailboards ☎ 202/333–4861 Paddle boats are available in summer on the east side of the Tidal Basin in front of the Jefferson Memorial ☎ 202/479–2426

GOLF

Washington has three public golf courses: **The Hains Point course** ✉ East Potomac Park near the Jefferson Memorial ☎ 202/554–7660 **Langston Golf Course** ✉ 26th Street and Benning Road NE ☎ 202/397–8638 **Rock Creek Park** ✉ 16th and Rittenhouse Streets NW ☎ 202/882–7332

Suburban public courses: **Reston National** ✉ 11875 Sunrise Valley Drive, Reston, VA ☎ 703/620–9333 **Northwest Park** ✉ 15701 Layhill Road, Wheaton, MD ☎ 301/598–6100 **Enterprise** ✉ 2802 Enterprise Road, Mitchellville, MD ☎ 301/249–2040

TENNIS

The District of Columbia has 144 outdoor courts. Send a self-addressed, stamped envelope or call the Department of Recreation for information, free permits and a list of courts. ✉ Department of Recreation, 3149 16th Street NW, 20010 ☎ 202/673–7646

Spectator sports

In addition to participant sports activities, Washington offers spectator sports. If you are here in autumn, you will hear about the Redskins, the football team, but season-ticket holders have all the seats. You'll have better luck seeing the Wizards play basketball or the Capitals play hockey, both at the MCI Center in downtown Washington. For tickets, call TicketMaster ☎ 202/432–7328.

LUXURY HOTELS

Prices

Expect to pay $180 or more for a double room in a luxury hotel (excluding tax, plus $1.50 per night occupancy tax).

Booking agencies

Capitol Reservations books rooms at over 70 better hotels at rates 20–40 percent lower than normal; call 202/452 1270 or 800/847 4832 weekdays 8:30–6:30; it also offers packages with tours and meals. Washington D.C. Accommodations will book rooms in any hotel in town, with discounts of 20–40 percent available at about 40 locations; call 202/289–2220 or 800/554–2220 weekdays 9–6.

FOUR SEASONS HOTEL

Located on the eastern edge of Georgetown, this hotel is known as a gathering place for Washington's elite.
E3 2800 Pennsylvania Avenue NW 202/342–0444 or 800/332–3442 (fax 202/342–1673) Foggy Bottom

HAY-ADAMS HOTEL

Looking like a mansion in disguise, this hotel has south-side rooms with a picture-postcard view of the White House. Rooms are decorated in English-country-house fashion.
F4 1 Lafayette Square NW 202/638–6600 or 800/424–5054 (fax 202/638–2716) McPherson Square

JEFERSON HOTEL

This small luxury hotel with outstanding service abounds with Federal-style finery.
F3 1200 16th Street NW 202/347–2200 or 800/368–5966 (fax 202/785–1505) Farragut North

PARK HYATT

A notable collection of modern art adorns this hotel. The rooms, a mix of traditional and contemporary styles, are accented with reproductions of Chinese antiques.
E3 1201 24th Street NW 202/ 789–1234 or 800/233–1234 (fax 202/457–8823) Foggy Bottom

THE RITZ-CARLTON

With European furnishings and 18th- and 19th-century English art, the decor is English hunt-club.
F3 2100 Massachusetts Avenue NW 202/293–2100 or 800/241– 3333 (fax 202/835–2196) Dupont Circle

RITZ-CARLTON, PENTAGON CITY

Just across the Potomac River from D.C., this hotel has a $2 million art and antiques collection displayed in its public areas. Many rooms have a view of the monuments across the river.
D8 1250 S Hayes Street Arlington, VA 703/415–5000 or 800/241–3333 (fax 703/415–5061) Pentagon City

STOUFFER RENAISSANCE MAYFLOWER

The ornate lobby glistens with gilded trim. The rooms feature custom designed furniture.
F4 1127 Connecticut Avenue NW 202/347–3000 or 800/468–3571 (fax 202/766–9184) Farragut North

WATERGATE HOTEL

Best known for its part in the fall of Richard Nixon, this hotel has large rooms; most have river views and many have balconies.
E4 2650 Virginia Avenue NW 202/965–2300 or 800/424–2736 (fax 202/337–7915) Foggy Bottom

WILLARD INTER-CONTINENTAL

Heads of state have made the Willard, steps from the White House, home since 1853. *Beaux-arts* lobby contrasts with staid rooms.
G4 1401 Pennsylvania Avenue NW 202/628–9100 or 800/327–0200 (fax 202/637–7326) McPherson Square

Moderately Priced Hotels

CAPITOL HILL SUITES
This all-suite hotel is tucked away behind the Madison Building of the Library of Congress.
J6 200 C Street SE 202/543–6000 or 800/424–9165 (fax 202/547–2608) Capitol South

DOUBLETREE GUEST SUITES
With two locations, these all-suite hotels are close to Georgetown and the Kennedy Center.
E4 801 New Hampshire Avenue NW 202/785–2000 or 800/424–2900 (fax 202/785–9485) Foggy Bottom; E4 2500 Pennsylvania Avenue NW 202/333–8060 or 800/424–2900 (fax 202/338–3818) Foggy Bottom

GEORGE WASHINGTON UNIVERSITY INN
This European-style eight-story hotel is only a few blocks from Georgetown. Half the rooms are suites.
E4 824 New Hampshire Avenue NW 202/337–6620 (fax 202/298–7499) Foggy Bottom

GEORGETOWN DUTCH INN
This all-suite hotel, on a side street in Georgetown, has a homey ambience.
D4 1075 Thomas Jefferson Street NW 202/337–0900 or 800/333–0124 (fax 202/333– 6526)

HENLEY PARK HOTEL
A bit of Britain in a developing neighborhood, this is a National Trust for Historic Preservation's designated Historic Hotel.
G4 926 Massachusetts Avenue NW 202/638–5200 or 800/222–8474 (fax 202/638–6740) Mt. Vernon Square–UDC

LATHAM HOTEL
This small, colonial-style hotel on one of Georgetown's main streets offers views of busy M Street or the C & O Canal. The popular Citronelle Restaurant is one of Washington's best.
D3 3000 M Street NW 202/726–5000 or 800/368–5922 (fax 202/337–4250)

MORRISON-CLARK INN HOTEL
Created by merging two 1864 townhouses, this inn is also one of the National Trust for Historic Preservation's designated Historic Hotels. The restaurant is highly rated.
G4 Massachusetts Avenue and 11th Street NW 202/898–1200 or 800/332–7898 (fax 202/289–8576) Mt. Vernon Square–UDC

NORMANDY INN
This European-style hotel is on a quiet street in the exclusive embassy area of Connecticut Avenue. Wine and cheese reception every Tuesday evening.
E2 2118 Wyoming Avenue NW 202/483–1350 or 800/424–3729 (fax 202/387–241)

RIVER INN
This small, all-suite hotel is steps from Georgetown, George Washington University, and the Kennedy Center. Rooms are homey and modest.
E4 924 25th Street NW 202/337–7600 or 800/424–2741 (fax 202/337–6520) Foggy Bottom

Prices

Expect to pay between $100 and $180 for a double room in a mid-range hotel (excluding tax, plus $1.50 per night occupancy tax).

Washington hotels

Most major chains have hotels in the city and the nearby suburbs. For a complete list of hotels, contact the Washington D.C. Convention and Visitors Association (1212 New York Avenue NW, Washington, D.C.. 20005 202/789–7000). All the hotels here are air-conditioned. Nearly all the finer hotels have superb restaurants whose traditionally high prices are almost completely justified.

Budget Accommodations

Prices

Expect to pay under $100 for a double room in budget accommodations (excluding tax, plus $1.50 per night occupancy tax).

Bed & breakfast

To find reasonably priced accommodations in small guest houses and private homes, contact either of the following bed-and-breakfast services: Bed 'n' Breakfast Accommodations Ltd. of Washington D.C. (✉ Box 12011, Washington, DC 20005 ☎ 202/328–3510); or Bed and Breakfast League, Ltd. (✉ Box 9490, Washington, DC 20016 9490 ☎ 202/363–7767). If you require a private bathroom, make this clear at the time of booking.

DAYS INN CONNECTICUT AVENUE

This standard hotel is away from the busy downtown area but only two blocks from the Metro.
Off map to north-west ✉ 4400 Connecticut Avenue NW ☎ 202/244–5600 or 800/325–2525 (fax 202/244–6794) Ⓜ Van Ness

HOLIDAY INN EISENHOWER

A bargain for the budget-minded traveler, located near the Old Town section of Alexandria.
Off map to south ✉ 2460 Eisenhower Avenue, Alexandria, VA ☎ 703/960–3400 or 800/465–4329 (fax 703/329–0953) Ⓜ Eisenhower

HOLIDAY INN ROSSLYN WESTPARK

This hotel is just across Key Bridge from Georgetown.
Off map to south ✉ 1900 N. Fort Ayer Drive, Arlington, VA ☎ 703/807–2000 or 800/465–4329 (fax 703/522–8864) Ⓜ Rosslyn

HOTEL TABARD INN

Consisting of three joined Victorian townhouses, the Tabard has charmingly well-worn furnishings.
F3 ✉ 1739 N Street NW ☎ 202/785–1277 (fax 202/785–6173) Ⓜ Dupont Circle

HOWARD JOHNSON'S EXPRESS INN

This is located on one of the main routes into the city.
K3 ✉ 600 New York Avenue NE ☎ 202/546–9200 or 800/446–4656 (fax 202/546–6348)

KALORAMA GUEST HOUSE

This inn consists of five separate turn-of-the-century townhouses, decorated with old-fashioned charm. No phones or TV. Complimentary breakfast and afternoon aperitifs.
F2 ✉ 1854 Mintwood Place NW ☎ 202/667–6369 (fax 202/319–1262); ✉ 2700 Cathedral Avenue NW ☎ 202/328–0860 (fax 202/328–8730)

THE PREMIER HOTEL

Located close to the Kennedy Center and Georgetown, this hotel offers large and comfortable rooms.
E4 ✉ 2601 Virginia Avenue NW ☎ 202/965–2700 or 800/965– 6869 (fax 202/337–5417 ext 7910) Ⓜ Foggy Bottom

WASHINGTON INTERNATIONAL AYH-HOSTEL

This well-kept hostel has dormitory rooms with 250 bunk beds; families are given their own rooms if the hostel is not full.
G4 ✉ 1009 11th Street NW ☎ 202/737– 2333 (fax 202/737–1508) Ⓜ McPherson Square

WINDSOR PARK HOTEL

Rooms in this small hotel are decorated with Queen Anne-style furnishings and period art. Each room has a small refrigerator. Free Continental breakfast.
E2 ✉ 2116 Kalorama Road NW ☎ 202/483– 7700 or 800/247–3064 (fax 202/332–4547)

WASHINGTON
travel facts

ARRIVING & DEPARTING

When to go

- In spring, the most crowded season, the city is alive with flowers and blossoming trees, including the must-see-to-believe cherry blossoms around the Tidal Basin and Washington Monument.

Climate

- Spring and autumn are lovely in Washington, with average high temperatures of between 59°F and 77°F.
- Summers are very hot and humid, with temperatures sometimes reaching 95°F or more.
- Winters are unpredictable: a year of record cold weather and below-freezing temperatures was recently followed by one of the warmest winters ever.
- Snowfall is equally unpredictable, but when snowstorms do occur, they tend to shut the city down.

Arriving by plane

- The major gateways to Washington, D.C., include **National Airport** ☎ 703/419–8000, in Virginia, 4 miles south of downtown Washington
  Dulles International Airport ☎ 703/572–2700, 26 miles west of Washington
  Baltimore-Washington International (BWI) Airport ☎ 410/859–7100, in Maryland, about 25 miles northeast of Washington.
  Flying time is one hour from New York, two hours from Chicago, and five hours, 40 minutes from Los Angeles.
- Major air carriers serving the three airports include
  Air Canada ☎ 800/776–3000
  Air France ☎ 800/237–2747
  All Nippon Airways ☎ 800/235– 9262
  America West ☎ 800/235–9292
  American Airlines ☎ 800/433–7300
  British Airways ☎ 800/247–9297
  Business Express ☎ 800/345–3400
  Continental ☎ 800/525–0280
  Delta ☎ 800/221–1212
  El Al ☎ 800/223–6700
  Icelandair ☎ 800/223–5500
  Japan Air Lines ☎ 800/525–3663
  KLM Royal Dutch ☎ 800/374–7747
  Lufthansa ☎ 800/645–3880
  Midwest Express ☎ 800/452–2022
  Northwest ☎ 800/225–2525
  Saudi Arabian Airlines ☎ 800/472–8342
  Swissair ☎ 800/221–4750
  TWA ☎ 800/221–2000
  United ☎ 800/241–6522
  USAir ☎ 800/428–4322
- For inexpensive, no-frills flights, contact **Midway** ☎ 888/226–4392 and **Valujet** ☎ 770/994–8258 or 800/825–8538).
- To register complaints about charter and scheduled airlines, contact the U.S. Department of Transportation's **Aviation Consumer Protection Division**, C-75, Rm. 1047, Washington D.C. 20590 ☎ 202/366–2220 or 800/322–7873).
- Established consolidators selling to the public include **Euram Flight Centre** ✉ 1522 K Street NW, Suite 430, Washington D.C., 20005 ☎ 800/848–6789 and **TFI Tours International** ✉ 34 W 32nd Street, New York, NY 10001 ☎ 212/736–1140 or 800/745–8000.
- Taxi to downtown: the fare for one person to downtown from National is about $13 (plus a $1.25 surcharge); from Dulles, $45; and from BWI, $50.

- Bus to downtown: Washington Flyer ☎ 703/685–1400 goes from Dulles airport to 1517 K Street, where a free shuttle bus serves several hotels. The 45-minute trip costs $16 ($26 round-trip). An inter-airport service between Dulles and National is available for about $16 ($26 round-trip). Pay with cash, MasterCard, or Visa; children under six ride free.
- SuperShuttle buses ☎ 800/809-7080 leave BWI hourly and National half-hourly for 1517 K Street NW. The 65-minute ride from BWI costs $21 ($31 round-trip); the 20-minute ride from National costs $8 ($14 round-trip); cash, traveler's checks and major credit cards accepted.

Train to downtown

- Free shuttle buses run between airline terminals and the train station at BWI airport.
- Amtrak (☎ 800/872–7245) and MARC (Maryland Rail Commuter Service ☎ 800/325-7245) trains run between BWI and Union Station from around 6AM to midnight.
- The cost of the 40-minute ride is $13 on Amtrak, $5 on MARC (weekdays only).

Limousine to downtown

- Diplomat Limousine (☎ 703/461–6800) will chauffeur you downtown from National, Dulles or BWI for $86.25, tip included. Book at least a day ahead.
- Private Car (☎ 800/685–0888) has a counter at BWI airport ($63 to downtown), or call ahead for a car to meet you at National ($45 to downtown) or Dulles ($75).
- Some hotels provide van service to and from the airports; check with your hotel.

ESSENTIAL FACTS

Travel insurance

- Travel insurance for baggage, health, and trip cancellation or interruptions is available from **Access America** ✉ Box 90315, Richmond, VA 23286 ☎ 804/285–3300 or 800/284–8300 **Carefree Travel Insurance** ✉ Box 9366, 100 Garden City Plaza, Garden City, NY 11530 ☎ 516/294–0220 or 800/323–3149 **Near Travel Services** ✉ Box 1339, Calumet City, IL 60409 ☎ 708/868–6700 or 800/654–6700 **Tele-Trip** ✉ Mutual of Omaha Plaza, Box 31716, Omaha, NE 68131 ☎ 800/228–9792 **Travel Insured International** ✉ Box 280568, East Hartford, CT 06128-0568 ☎ 203/528–7663 or 800/243–3174 **Travel Guard International** ✉ 1145 Clark Street, Stevens Point, WI 54481 ☎ 715/345–0505 or 800/826–1300 **Wallach & Company** ✉ 107 W Federal Street, Box 480, Middleburg, VA 22117 ☎ 703/687–3166 or 800/237–6615

Opening hours

- Stores: Mon–Sat 10–7 (or 8). Some have extended hours on Thursday; those in shopping or tourist areas often open Sunday 10 or noon–5 or 6.
- Banks: Mon–Fri 9–3. Some stay open until 5 on Friday, or close at 2 and open again 4–6.
- Museums: daily 10–5:30; some have extended hours on Thursday. Many private museums are closed Monday or Tuesday and some museums in government office buildings are closed weekends. The Smithsonian often sets extended spring and summer hours

annually for some of its museums. ☎ 202/357–2700 for details.

Public holidays

- New Year's Day (January 1)
- Martin Luther King Day (third Monday in January)
- Presidents Day (third Monday in February)
- Memorial Day (last Monday in May)
- Independence Day (July 4)
- Labor Day (the first Monday in September)
- Veterans' Day (November 11)
- Thanksgiving Day (the fourth Thursday in November)
- Christmas Day (December 25)
- Banks, post offices, and most government agencies are closed for these holidays, although most museums and stores are open.

Money matters

- You can use your bank card at ATMs to withdraw money from an account and get cash advances on a credit-card account if your card has been programmed with a personal identification number, or PIN. Before leaving home, check on frequency limits for withdrawals and cash advances.
- On cash advances you are charged interest from the day you receive the money from ATMs as well as from tellers. Transaction fees for ATM withdrawals outside your home turf may be higher than for withdrawals at home.
- Money transfer: you can send or receive a MoneyGram from American Express (☎ 800/926–9400) for up to $20,000. MoneyGram agents are in more than 70 countries. Western Union (☎ 800/325–6000) is linked to 22,000 locations in more than 100 countries.

Places of worship

- Episcopal: Washington National Cathedral ✉ Wisconsin and Massachusetts Avenues NW ☎ 202/537–6200)
- Jewish: Adas Israel ✉ Connecticut Avenue and Porter Street NW ☎ 202/362–4433
- Muslim: Islamic Mosque and Cultural Center ✉ 2551 Massachusetts Avenue NW ☎ 202/332–8343)
- Roman Catholic: National Shrine of the Immaculate Conception, ✉ Michigan Avenue and 4th Street NE ☎ 202/526–8300 Franciscan Monastery ✉ 14th and Quincy Streets NE ☎ 202/526–6800.

Toilets

- Finding rest rooms can be difficult in Washington.
- There are facilities on the Mall around and west of the Washington Monument as well as in all the museums.
- There are no public facilities in downtown or shopping areas.
- Fast food restaurants generally have rest rooms, but you might have to ask for a key or a token to open the door.

Time

- For the current time ☎ 202/844–2525

Public Transportation

- The subway (Metro) and bus (Metrobus) systems are run by the Washington Metropolitan

Area Transit Authority (WMATA).

- Maps of the Metro system and some bus schedules are available in all Metro stations or at WMATA headquarters ✉ 600 5th Street NW.
- For general information or a copy of "Welcome Aboard," a helpful brochure, ☎ 202/637–7000 weekdays 6AM–10:30PM; weekends 8AM–10:30PM; Consumer assistance ☎ 202/637–1328. Transit police ☎ 202/962–2121.

The Metro

- The city's 20-year-old subway system, the Metro, is one of the cleanest and safest in the country.
- Trains run every few minutes, Mon–Fri 5:30AM–midnight, Sat and Sun 8AM–midnight.
- The basic fare ($1.10) goes up based on how far you are going and the time of day you are riding (fares are higher during rush hours, 5:30–9:30AM and 3–8PM). Maps in the stations tell you both the rush hour fare and regular fare to any destination station.
- You need a farecard to ride the Metro, both to enter and to exit. Farecard machines, located in the stations, take coins and $1, $5, $10, and $20 bills (the most change the machine will give you is about $5, so don't use a large bill if you are buying a low-value card).
- Insert your farecard into the slot on the side of the turnstile. Retrieve it once the gate opens as you will need it to exit. On exiting, insert the farecard into the turnstile. If your card is for the exact fare the gate will open and you can exit; if your card still has some money on it, it will again pop out the top of the turnstile. A red "STOP" light means you need more money on your card to leave the station and must go the Addfare machine; insert your card and the machine will tell you how much additional fare is owed; pay that fare and return to the exit turnstile.
- The farecards are reusable until the card has a value of less than $1.10. Then, should you need another farecard, your old card can be used as cash in the farecard machine by putting it in the "Used Farecard Trade-In" slot.
- A $5 one-day pass is available for unlimited trips on weekends, holidays or after 9:30AM weekdays. These passes are available at Metro Sales Outlets, including the Metro Center station and some hotels, banks, and grocery stores.
- If you plan to transfer to a bus upon leaving the Metro, get a transfer (before boarding your train) from the dispenser located next to the escalator that goes down to the train level.

Buses

- The bus system covers a much wider area than does the Metro.
- The fare within the city is $1.10.
- Free bus-to-bus transfers are available from the driver and are good for about 2 hours at designated Metrobus transfer points.

Taxis

- Taxi fares are based on a somewhat hard-to-understand zone system. Maps showing the zones must be displayed in all cabs but even so it is still difficult to know when you are in which zone.

- The base fare for one passenger within a zone is $4, with a $1.25 charge for each extra passenger and a $1 surcharge Mon–Fri 4–6:30PM.
- If you think that you have been overcharged, ask for the driver's name and cab number and then threaten to call the D.C. Taxicab Commission ☎ 202/645 6018.

Car rental

- Alamo ☎ 800/327–9633
- Avis ☎ 800/331–1212, 800/879–2847 in Canada
- Budget ☎ 800/527–0700
- Dollar ☎ 800/800–4000
- Hertz ☎ 800/654–3131, 800/263–0600 in Canada
- National ☎ 800/227–7368

MEDIA & COMMUNICATIONS

Telephones

- Local telephone calls (including nearby suburbs) cost 25 cents.
- There are three local area codes:
  202 (Washington)
  301 (Maryland, except numbers in Baltimore which are prefixed by 410), and
  703 (Virginia)
- The local access numbers for AT&T, MCI, and Sprint are as follows:
  AT&T 1–800–CALLATT
  MCI 10222
  Sprint 1–800–877–8000
- Information ☎ 411 (calls are usually free)
- Police or medical emergency ☎ 911

Post offices

- The National Postal Museum (Massachusetts Avenue and North Capitol Street NE), next door to Union Station, is a working post office.
- Other branches include
  Farragut ✉ 1145 19th Street NW ☎ 202/523–2506
  Georgetown ✉ 1215 31st Street NW ☎ 202/523–2405
  L'Enfant Plaza ✉ 458 L'Enfant Plaza SW ☎ 202/523–2013
  Washington Square ✉ 1050 Connecticut Avenue NW ☎ 202/523–2631

Newspapers

- Washington has two major daily newspapers, *The Washington Post* and the *Washington Times*.
- In addition, there are various neighborhood weekly newspapers serving Capitol Hill, Georgetown, Adams-Morgan and other areas.
- The *City Paper*, a free weekly with an emphasis on entertainment, is available from newspaper boxes around town and at many restaurants, clubs and other outlets.
- The *Washington Blade*, a free weekly aimed at gays and lesbians, is available at many restaurants, bars and stores, especially in the Dupont Circle, Adams-Morgan, and Capitol Hill areas, or at Lambda Rising ✉ 1625 Connecticut Avenue NW ☎ 202/462–6969 or Lammas ✉ 1426 21st Street NW ☎ 202/775–8218.
- *Washingtonian*, a monthly magazine, has a calendar of events, dining information, and articles about the city or prominent people here.
- *Where/Washington* is a monthly magazine (free at most hotels) listing popular things to do. If your hotel doesn't have a copy ☎ 202/463–4550.
- Other national newspapers are available at newspaper boxes.

Emergencies

Sensible precautions

- Washington's reputation as a dangerous city is somewhat unfair — it is approximately as safe as any medium-to-large city anywhere. Violent crime is mainly concentrated far from the downtown and tourist areas, in sections of the city you are unlikely to visit.
- Use the same precautions you would use in any city: at night, or on quiet streets, always be aware of what's going on around you; if possible, walk with someone rather than alone; it is wise to use taxis for traveling to less populous areas at night.
- Should you be attacked, co-operate, then immediately call the police on 911.

Lost property

- Metro or Metrobus: ☎ 202/962–1195
- Smithsonian museums: ☎ 202/357–2700
- Other lost articles: check with the police at ☎ 202/727–1010.

Medical treatment

- Dial 911 for assistance.
- The hospital closest to downtown is George Washington University Hospital (✉ 901 23rd Street NW ☎ 202/994–3211, emergencies only).
- 1–800–DOCTORS (☎ 800/362–8677) is a referral service that locates doctors, dentists and urgent-care clinics in the greater Washington area.
- The D.C. Dental Society (☎ 202/547–7615) operates a referral line weekdays 8–4.

Medicines

- Late-night pharmacies: CVS Pharmacy operates 24-hour pharmacies at 14th Street and Thomas Circle NW ☎ 202/628–0720 and at 7 Dupont Circle NW ☎ 202/785–1466 .

Visitor Information

- Contact the **Washington D.C. Convention and Visitors Association** (✉ 1212 New York Ave. NW, 6th Floor, Washington, DC 20005 ☎ 202/789–7000, fax 202/789–7037); the **D.C. Committee to Promote Washington** (✉ 1212 New York Ave. NW, 2nd Floor, Washington, DC 20005 ☎ 800/422–8644); or the **National Park Service** (✉ Office of Public Affairs, National Capital Region, 1100 Ohio Dr. SW, Washington, DC 20242 ☎ 202/619–7222)
- The **White House Visitor Center** ☎ 202/208–1631, in Baldridge Hall in the Department of Commerce Building (✉ 1450 Pennsylvania Avenue NW), has information on White House tours and special events.
  National Park Service information kiosks on the Mall, near the White House, next to the Vietnam Veterans Memorial, and at several other locations throughout the city, can provide helpful information.
  Dial-A-Park ☎ 202/619–7275 is a recording of events at Park Service attractions in and around Washington.
  Dial-A-Museum ☎ 202/357–2020 is a recording of exhibits and special offerings at Smithsonian Institution museums.

INDEX

Citypack *Washington, D.C.*

Published in the United States by Fodor's Travel Publications, Inc.
Published in the United Kingdom by AA Publishing

Fodor's is a registered trademark of Fodor's Travel Publications, Inc.

ISBN 0-679-00006-2
Second Edition

FODOR'S CITYPACK WASHINGTON, D.C.

AUTHORS *Mary Case and Bruce Walker*
CARTOGRAPHY *The Automobile Association*
RV Reise- und Verkehrsverlag
COVER DESIGN *Tigist Getachew, Fabrizio La Rocca*
COPY EDITOR *Beth Ingpen*
VERIFIER *Judy Sykes*
INDEXER *Marie Lorimer*
SECOND EDITION UPDATED BY *OutHouse Publishing Services*

Acknowledgments

The Automobile Association would like to thank the following photographers, libraries, and associations for their assistance in the preparation of this book: M GOSTELOW 7, 57; THE PHILLIPS COLLECTION 27; PICTURES COLOUR LIBRARY LTD 13a; SPECTRUM COLOUR LIBRARY 13b, 41b.

All remaining pictures were taken by Ethel Davies and are held in the Automobile Association's own library (AA PHOTO LIBRARY).

Color separation by Daylight Colour Art Pte Ltd, Singapore
Manufactured by Dai Nippon Printing Co. (Hong Kong) Ltd
10 9 8 7 6 5 4 3 2 1

Titles in the Citypack series

• Amsterdam • Atlanta • Berlin • Boston • Chicago • Florence • Hong Kong •
• London • Los Angeles • Miami • Montréal • New York • Paris • Prague •
• Rome • San Francisco • Tokyo • Toronto • Venice • Washington, D.C. •